Hans Christian Andersen's Fairy Tales

Life itself is the most wonderful fairy tale

7

"Life itself is the most wonderful fairy tale."

CONTENTS

THE PORTER'S SON
(1866)

The General's family lived on the first floor, and the Porter's family lived in the cellar. There was a vast distance between them—the whole first floor, as well as all the grades of society; but both families lived under the same roof, and their windows looked out in the same street and the same garden.

In this garden there was a blooming acacia—whenever it did bloom—and sometimes the smartly dressed nurse would sit under it with the still more smartly dressed child, the General's "Little Emilie."

The Porter's little son, with his dark hair and large brown eyes, used to dance barefoot before them; and the little girl would laugh and stretch her tiny hands out to him. And if the General saw this from his window he would nod down at them and say, "Charmant!" The General's wife, who was so young that she might almost have been her husband's daughter by an earlier marriage, never herself looked out into the yard; but she had given orders that the Porter's boy could play near her own child, but never touch it. And the nurse strictly carried out the lady's orders.

The sun shone in upon those who dwelt on the first floor and those who lived in the cellar. The acacia put out its blossoms, they fell away, and new ones came the next year. The tree bloomed, and the Porter's little son bloomed; he looked like a fresh tulip.

The General's little daughter grew to be a delicate child, as dainty as the rosy petal of the acacia blossom. Now she seldom sat under the tree, for she took the fresh air in a carriage, She went with her mother on drives, and always nodded to the Porter's son, George; yes, and even kissed her fingers toward him, till her mother told her she was now too grown-up for that.

One morning he had to bring the General some papers and mail that had been left in the Porter's room. He had mounted the staircase and was passing the door of the broom closet when he heard a peep from inside it. He thought perhaps it was a stray chicken chirping, but it was the General's little daughter, dressed in muslin and lace.

"Don't tell Papa and Mamma, for they would be angry!"

"What's the matter, little lady?" asked George.

"It's all burning everywhere!" she said. "It's in full blaze!"

George flung open the door to the little nursery, where the window curtain was nearly all burned; the curtain rod had caught fire and was flaming! Quickly he sprang forward, pulled it down, and called for help: without him the whole house would have caught fire.

The General and his wife questioned Little Emilie.

"I just took only one single match," she said, "and that lighted up and then the whole curtain lighted up! I spit to put out the fire; I spit all I could, but I didn't have enough spit, so I came out and hid, 'cause I knew Papa and Mamma would be angry!"

"Spit!" said the General. "What sort of word is that? When did you ever hear your papa or your mamma talk of spitting? You must have learned that word downstairs!"

But little George received a penny. It didn't go to the candy store, but into his savings bank, and there were soon so many pennies there that he could buy himself a paintbox and color his drawings.

He had many of these drawings, for they seemed to come out of his very pencil and finger tips. He presented the first colored pictures to Little Emilie.

"Charmant!" said the General.

The General's wife admitted that it was quite clear what the little one meant in his pictures.

"There's genius in him!"

Those were the words the Porter's wife brought back down into the cellar.

The General and his lady were of the nobility; they had two coats of arms on their carriage, one for each of them. The lady had a crest worked on every piece of clothing, inside and outside, in her nightcap, and even on her night cover. This, her own coat of arms, was an expensive one, bought by her father for bright dollars, for he hadn't been born with it, and neither had she.

She had come into the world seven years before the crest, a fact that was remembered by most people, though forgotten by the family. The General's coat of arms was old and large; one's back might well creak with dignity of this one alone, to say nothing of the two of them. And there was indeed a creaking in the lady's back when she drove stiff and stately to the court balls.

The General was old and gray, but he knew how to sit on a horse, and rode out every day, with a groom at a respectful distance behind him. When he arrived at a party it was as if he had ridden into the room on his high horse, and he wore so many decorations that it was almost unbelievable, but that was by no means his fault. When a very young man he had performed military duties by taking part in the great autumnal war games that used to be held in times of peace. He always told an anecdote of those days—his only one. The officer under him cut off and captured one of the princes; and the prince and his little troop, all prisoners like himself, had to ride back to towns behind the General. It was an event never to be forgotten, and the General told it again and again, year after year, always ending with the remarkable words he had spoken when he returned the prince's sword to him: "Only my subaltern officer could have made your Royal Highness a prisoner; I—never!" Whereupon the prince had answered, "You are incomparable!"

The General had never seen active service, for when war came to his native land he went on diplomatic missions, through three foreign countries. He spoke French until he had almost forgotten his own language; he danced beautifully, and he rode well; decorations blossomed on his blouse in indescribable abundance; sentinels presented arms to him; one of the prettiest of the girls presented herself to him—and became his wife. And they had a lovely little girl, so pretty that she seemed to have fallen from Heaven; and the Porter's son danced in the garden before her as soon as she was old enough to take notice, and gave her all his colored drawings; and she looked at them and was so delighted with them that she tore them to pieces. She was so beautiful and charming.

"My rose petal!" said the General's wife. "You were born to be the bride of a prince!" The prince was already standing outside the door, but no one knew it. People can't see much farther than the doorstep.

"The other day our boy shared his bread and butter with her," said the Porter's wife. "There was neither cheese nor meat with it, but she enjoyed it every bit as much as roast beef. There'd have been a fine hullabaloo if the General and his wife had seen that little party, but they didn't!"

George had shared his bread and butter with Little Emilie, and gladly would he have shared his very heart with her, if only it would have pleased her. He was a good boy, wide-awake and intelligent, and now he was studying drawing at the evening school at the academy. Little Emilie, too, was advancing in learning; she talked French and had a dancing master.

"George is going to be confirmed at Easter," said the Porter's wife. That was how far George was advanced.

"It would be very sensible to have him serve an apprenticeship," said the father; "in some good profession, of course; and then we would have him out of the house!"

"But he could come home at nights to sleep," said the mother.

"It wouldn't be easy to find a master who had a spare room. And we'd have to give him clothes, too; the little food he eats now we can easily afford to give him; he is happy with a couple of boiled potatoes; then he has his teaching free. Just let him go on the way he is, and he'll turn out a blessing to us, you may be sure! Didn't the professor say so?"

The confirmation clothes were ready. Mother did the sewing herself, but the cloth had been cut by the tailor, and he knew how to cut it. The Porter's wife said that if he had only been better placed, and could have opened a shop with apprentices, he could have become court tailor.

Yes, the clothes were ready, and the candidate was ready. On confirmation day George received a great pocket watch from his godfather, the flax dealer's old clerk, the wealthiest of George's godfathers. The watch was old and honored; it was always a little fast, but that's better than being too slow. It was a precious present. And from the General's there came a hymnbook bound in leather, sent by the little lady to whom George had given his pictures. On the flyleaf were written his name and her name as "his gracious well-wisher." This was written according to the dictation of the General's wife, and the General himself had read it through and said, "Charmant!"

"That was really a great courtesy from a family of such rank," said the Porter's wife. And George would have to go upstairs, in his confirmation clothes and carrying his hymnbook, to thank them.

The General's wife had a number of compresses on her head, for she had one of her bad headaches, which always came when she was bored. She looked very kindly at George and wished him the best of luck and none of her headaches.

The General was wearing his dressing gown, with a tasseled cap and red-legged Russian boots. He paced up and down the floor three times, engrossed in his own thoughts and memories. Then he stood still and said, "So now little George is a Christian man! Let him be also an honest man, paying due respect to his government! Someday, when you are old, you can say the General taught you that sentence." That was a much longer speech than the General usually made; and he returned to his inner thoughts and looked impressive.

But George heard and saw little of all that up there; nothing remained fixed in his memory so firmly as little Miss Emilie.

How lovely she was, and how gentle; how she flitted about, and how delicate she was! If one should draw her portrait it would have to be in a soap bubble. There was a fragrance about her clothing and her curly blonde hair as if she were a rosebush that had just burst into bloom. And he had once shared his bread and butter with her, and she had eaten it with a huge appetite and smiled at him with every second mouthful. Could she possibly still remember it? Surely she did; it was in memory of this that she had given him the beautiful hymnbook.

And so, on New Year's Day, just as the new moon of the new year rose, he went out of doors with a loaf and a shilling and opened the book at random to see what hymn should appear. It was a song of praise and thanksgiving. Then he opened it again to see what should come forth for Little Emilie. He tried very hard not to dip into the part of the book containing the funeral hymns, but in spite of his care he did dip in between death and the grave. You couldn't believe in that sort of thing—not in the least! And yet he was terribly frightened when soon afterward the dainty little girl was laid up with sickness and the doctor's carriage came to the street door daily.

"They won't be able to keep her," said the Porter's wife. "Our Lord knows very well whom He wants."

But they kept her, and George sent her pictures he drew. He drew the Czar's palace, the ancient Kremlin in Moscow, exactly as it was, with turrets and cupolas; in George's drawing they looked like big green and gilt cucumbers. Little Emilie was so pleased that during the week George sent her several more pictures, all of buildings, because that would give her plenty to think about, wondering what went on inside the doors and windows.

He drew a Chinese house, with bells hanging on all the sixteen stories. He drew two Greek temples, with steps around slender marble pillars. He drew a Norwegian church; you could see it was made entirely of timbers, deeply carved and curiously put together; every story looked as if it had rockers. But the most beautiful design of all was a castle, which he called "Little Emilie's." This was to be her own home, so George had made it all up from his imagination and selected for it whatever seemed prettiest in each of the other buildings. It had the carved beams of the Norwegian church, the marble pillars of the Greek temples, bells on every story, and green and gilded cupolas on the top, like those on the Czar's Kremlin. It was a true child's castle! And under every window was written what took place in that hall or that room: "Here Emilie sleeps": "Here Emilie dances"; and "Here she is to play 'visitors coming.'" It was amusing to look at, and you may be sure it was looked at. "Charmant!" said the General.

But the old Count—for there was an old count, of even greater distinction than the General, with a castle and a mansion of his own—said nothing. They had told him that all this had been imagined and drawn by the little son of the Porter. Not that the boy was so very little now; indeed, he had been confirmed. The old Count looked carefully at the pictures and had his own long, quiet thoughts about them.

One gray, damp, and dismal morning proved one of the brightest and best days for little George. The professor at the art academy sent for him.

"Listen, my friend," he said. "Let's have a little talk together. Our Lord has favored you with good talent; now He's favoring you with good friends. The old Count in the corner house has spoken to me about you. I have seen your pictures, too; frankly, those we can cross out, for there would be too much to correct in them. From now on you may come twice a week to my drawing school, and so in time you'll learn to do better. I believe there is more of the architect in you than of the painter. You will have time to think about this, but now go up right away to the old Count on the corner and thank the good Lord for such a friend."

It was a great mansion, that corner house! Carved figures of elephants and camels of the olden days were around the windows, but the Count was fonder of modern times, and anything good they brought, whether from drawing room, cellar, or garret.

"I believe," said the Porter's wife, "that the grander folks really are the less stuck-up they are. How kind and plain the old Count is! And he can talk just like you and me! You won't find that at the General's. There was George yesterday, head over heels with delight, because the Count treated him so graciously; and I'm much the same way today, after talking with that great man. Wasn't it lucky now that we didn't have George serve an apprenticeship? That boy has talent."

"But he must have outside help," said the father.

"Well, he's got that help now," said the mother. "The Count spoke right out, plain and honest."

"But it was at the General's that it was all started," said the father. "We must thank them, too."

"We can do that, too," said the mother, "though there's not much to thank them for, in my opinion. I'll thank our Lord first of all, and thank Him all the more now that Little Emilie is getting better again."

Emilie kept getting better, and George kept getting better; inside of a year he won the small silver medal, and later the large one.

"It would have been better, after all, if he had learned a trade!" said the Porter's wife, and cried. "We would have kept him here then. Why does he have to go off to Rome? I shall never see him any more, even if he comes home again, and that he'll never do, the sweet child!"

"But it's to his good fortune and glory," said the father.

"Ah, it's all very well to talk that way, my friend!" said the mother. "You talk, but you don't mean a word of it. You're just as heartbroken as I am!"

And it was all true, both about the sorrow and the departure. It was, however, a great piece of luck for the young man, said everyone.

And then there was a round of farewells, also at the General's. His wife did not appear, for she had one of her bad headaches. At parting the General related his only anecdote—what he had said to the prince, and how the prince had replied to him, "You are incomparable!" Then he gave George his hand, a flabby old hand.

Emilie gave George her hand, too, and looked almost sad; but George was the saddest.

Time passes when one is busy, but it also passes when one is idle. The time is equally long, though not equally profitable. It was profitable to George, and never seemed long, except when he thought of those at home and how they were getting along, in the drawing room and in the cellar. Yes, he had news of them, and a great deal may be folded up in a letter—bright sunshine and dark, heavy days. One letter told that his father had died, and so his mother was alone now. Emilie had been an angel of comfort at the time, having come down to her, wrote his mother. And as for herself, she added, she had received permission to keep her husband's job.

The General's wife kept a diary; in it were entered every ball, every party she had attended, every visit she had paid or received. The diary was illustrated with the cards of diplomats and other noblemen. She was very proud of her diary; it increased in size season after season, through many great headaches, but also through many bright evenings—that is, court balls.

Emilie went to her first court ball. Her mother wore pink, with black Spanish lace, while Emilie's dress was white, so fine and pure! Green ribbons fluttered like leaves in her curly blonde locks, and she was crowned with a wreath of white water lilies. Her eyes were so blue and clear, her mouth so beautiful and red; she looked like a little mermaid, as beautiful as you could imagine. Three princes danced with her; that is, one after the other. Her mother had no headache for a week.

But the first ball wasn't the last of the season. The pace became too much for Emilie, and so it was well that summer brought rest and a change of air. The family was invited to the old Count's castle.

The garden of this castle was worth seeing. A part of it was quite old-fashioned, with stiff green hedges, where one seemed to be walking between green screens pierced with peepholes. Box trees and yew trees were clipped into stars and pyramids; water sprang from fountains set with cockleshells; on all sides stood figures made of the heaviest stone, as one could plainly tell from both the clothes and the faces; each flower bed had its own device—a fish, a heraldic shield, or a monogram. This was the French part of the garden. From this section one seemed to emerge into the free, natural woods, where the trees could grow as they wished, and therefore, grew great and splendid. The grass was green and could be walked on; it was mowed, rolled, and well cared for. This was the English half of the garden.

"Old times and modern times," said the Count. "They meet here with loving embraces! In a couple of years the house itself will take on its proper importance. It will be a complete change into something handsomer and better. I'll show you the plans, and I'll even show you the architect; he is coming to dinner."

"Charmant!" said the General. "This garden is paradise!" said the General's wife. "And over there you have a baronial castle!"

"Oh, that's my henhouse," replied the Count. "The pigeons live in the tower, and the turkeys on the first floor, but old Else reigns in the parlor. She has guest rooms all around her, one for the sitting hens, one for the hens and chickens, while the ducks have their own outlet to the water."

"Charmant!" repeated the General, and they all went to see this fine place.

Old Else stood in the middle of the parlor, and beside her stood the architect—George! After so many years, he and Little Emilie met again—in the henhouse! Yes, there he stood, and he was a handsome figure to look at, his face frank and firm, his hair black and shiny, and in the corners of his mouth a little smile that said, "There's a little imp behind my ear who knows all about you, outside and inside!" Old Else had taken off her wooden shoes and stood in her stocking feet, out of respect for her illustrious visitors. And the hens clucked, and the cock crowed, while the ducks waddled along, tap, tap, tap.

But the pale, slender girl, his childhood friend, the General's daughter, stood before George with her otherwise pallid cheeks now blushing like the rose, her eyes wide, and her lips speaking without uttering a syllable. Such was his greeting—the sweetest that any young man could hope for from a young lady, unless they were of the same family or had often danced together; she and the architect had never danced together.

The Count took his hand and presented him, saying, "He's not a perfect stranger, our young friend, Mr. George."

The General's wife curtsied; her daughter was about to offer her hand, but drew it back.

"Our little Mr. George!" said the General. "We're old house-friends; charmant!"

"You have become quite an Italian," said his wife, "and I presume you speak the language now like a native."

The General's wife could sing in Italian but not speak it, said the General.

At the dinner table George sat at Emilie's right side. The General had escorted her, while the Count had escorted the General's wife. George talked, and told anecdotes, which he could tell well. He was the life of the party, though the old Count could have been, too, had he wanted to be.

Emilie sat silently; her ears listened, her eyes sparkled—but she said nothing.

Then she and George stood among the flowers, behind a screen of roses on the veranda, and again it was left to him to begin speaking.

"Thank you for your kindness to my old mother," he said. "I know that on the night of my father's death you went down and stayed with her till his eyes had closed. Thank you!" Then he raised her hand and kissed it, as was proper on such an occasion. She blushed, becoming rosy red, but pressed his hand in return and gazed at him with tender blue eyes.

"Your mother was a loving soul, and she was so fond of you. She let me read all your letters, so I almost feel I know you. And I remember how kind you were to me when I was little. You gave me pictures—"

"Which you tore to pieces," said George.

"No, I still have my own castle left—I mean the drawing of it."

"And now I must really build it!" said George, and grew quite excited himself as he said it.

In their own rooms the General and his wife talked about the Porter's son. Why, he knew how to carry himself and to speak with knowledge and refinement. "He could be a tutor," said the General.

"Genius!" said the General's wife, and that was all she did say.

Often during those fine summer days George came to the castle of the Count. They missed him when he didn't come.

"How much more our Lord has given to you than to us ordinary beings!" Emilie said to him. "Are you grateful for it now?"

George was flattered that this beautiful young girl should look up to him. He found her very gifted.

And the General was more and more convinced that Mr. George could hardly have been a real child of the cellar. "However, his mother was a mighty fine woman," he said; "I owe her that sentence as an epitaph!"

Summer passed, winter came, and there was still more to tell about Mr. George. He had received attention and favor in the highest of all highest places. The General had met him at the court ball!

And now there was a ball planned at home for Little Emilie. Could Mr. George be invited?

"Whom the King invites, the General can invite!" said the General, drawing himself up a good inch higher.

So Mr. George was invited, and he came. And princes and counts came, and each danced better than the other. But Emilie danced only the first dance, for during that she strained her ankle, not seriously but painfully, so she had to stop dancing and watch the others. And there she sat, looking on, while the architect stood beside her.

"You're giving her the whole of St. Peter's Church at Rome!" said the General as he passed, smiling like good humor itself.

A few days later he received Mr. George with the same smile of good humor. The young man had come to thank him for the ball, of course, and had he anything else to say? Yes—and the most surprising, astonishing, insane words were uttered by him. The General could hardly believe his ears. A preposterous declamation, an unbelievable proposition! Mr. George actually asked for Emilie as his wife!

"Man!" said the General as he began to boil. "I cannot understand you! What are you saying? What do you want? I don't know you! Sir! Fellow! You come and break into my house! Am I to remain here or am I not?" And then he backed into his bedroom, turned the key, and let Mr George stand alone. He stood there for a few moments, then turned around and left.

In the hallway he met Emilie. "What did my father say?" she asked in a trembling voice.

George pressed her hand. "He ran away from me—a better time will come."

There were tears in Emilie's eyes, while in the young man's were courage and confidence; the sun shone in upon them both and blessed them.

In his bedroom the General sat boiling; yes, still boiling—and then he boiled over and spluttered, "Lunacy! Porter madness!"

Inside of an hour the General's wife had heard it all from the General himself, and she sent for Emilie, to be alone with her. "Poor girl," she said. "To think of his insulting you like that, insulting all of us! I see there are tears in yours eyes; they're quite becoming to you. You really look charming in tears; you remind me of myself on my wedding day. Go ahead, cry, Little Emilie."

"Yes, that I certainly shall," said Emilie, "unless you and Papa say 'yes'!"

"Child!" cried the General's wife. "You're ill! You're delirious, and I'm getting one of my dreadful headaches! Oh, the miseries that are descending upon our house! Don't let your mother die, Emilie, because then you'll have no mother!" And her eyes filled with tears; she couldn't bear to consider her own death.

Among the notices of appointments to be read in the news paper was the following: "Mr. George has been appointed Professor, 5th Class, No. 8."

"What a shame his father and mother are dead and can't

read that!" said the new porters who now lived in the cellar under the General. They knew that the Professor had been born and brought up within those four walls.

"Now he'll have to pay the title tax!" said the man.

"Now, isn't that a lot for a poor child!" said the wife.

"Eighteen rix-dollars a year!" said the man. "Yes, that's a lot of money."

"No, I'm talking about the title!" said the wife. "You don't suppose having to pay the tax will worry him! He can earn that money many times over, and he'll probably marry a rich wife as well. If we had children, husband, a child of ours would also be an architect and a professor!"

Thus George was well spoken of in the cellar. He was well spoken of on the first floor, too; the old Count took good care of that.

It was the old drawings from his childhood days that presented an occasion for speaking about him. But how did these come to be mentioned? There was talk of Russia and Moscow, and so, of course, this brought one right to the Kremlin, of which little George had made that drawing for little Miss Emilie. How many pictures he used to draw! There was one the Count especially remembered—"Little Emilie's Castle," with signs showing where she slept, where she danced, and where she played "visitors coming." Yes, the Professor had great talent. He might someday become an old privy councillor—that wasn't at all unlikely—and build a real castle for the young lady before he died; why not?

"That was a strange form of gaiety," said the General's wife after the Count had gone. The General nodded thoughtfully and then went out riding, with the groom a respectful distance behind him, and he sat prouder than ever on his high horse.

Little Emilie's birthday brought cards and notes, books and flowers. The General kissed her on the brow, and his wife kissed her on the lips. They were loving parents, and both they and Emilie were honored with noble visitors—even two of the princes. Then there was much talk about balls and theaters, about diplomatic embassies, and the governments of kingdoms and empires. Then the talk turned on rising young men and native talent, and this brought the name of the young Professor into the conversation—Mr. Architect George.

"He is building for immortality," someone said. "And meanwhile he is building himself into one of the first families!"

"One of the first families!" repeated the General when he was alone with his wife. "Which one of our first families!"

"I can guess which was meant," said the General's wife. "But I won't speak of it or even think about it. God may have ordained it so, but I will be very surprised if he has!"

"Let me be surprised, too!" said the General. "I haven't an idea in my head!" Then he sank into a reverie, waiting for an idea to come.

There is a power, an unspeakable power, granted to a man by a few drops of grace from above—the grace of kings, the grace of God—and both of these were granted to little George.

But we are forgetting the birthday.

Emilie's room was fragrant with flowers from her friends and playmates. On her table lay fine presents, tokens of greeting and remembrance, but not one came from George. A gift from him would not have reached her, but it was not needed, for the whole house was a souvenir of him. A memorial flower peeped out from the broom closet under the stairs, where Emilie had peeped out when the curtain was burning and George had rushed up as first fireman. When she glanced from the window the acacia tree reminded her of childhood days. The blossoms and leaves were gone, but the tree stood shrouded in frost, like a great branch of coral, and the moon shone big and clear through the branches, unchanged though ever-changing, just as it was when George shared his bread and butter with Little Emilie.

From a drawer she took out the drawings of the Czar's Kremlin and her own castle remembrances from George. As she looked at them and mused over them, many thoughts arose in her mind. She remembered the day when, unnoticed by father or mother, she had stolen down to where the Porter's wife lay on her deathbed; she had sat by her side, held her hand, and heard her last words, "Blessings—George!" The mother's thoughts had been of her son. But now the words seemed to Emilie to carry a deeper meaning. In truth, George was with her on her birthday.

It so happened that the next day there was another birthday in the house, the General's, for he had been born the day after his daughter—naturally, many years earlier. Again there were presents, and among them a splendid—looking saddle, extremely comfortable and expensive; its only duplicate belonged to one of the princes. Who could have sent it? The General was in ecstasy. If the little card with it had said, "Thanks for yesterday," we could all guess where it came from, but the card said, "From one whom the General does not know."

"Who in the world is there I don't know?" said the General. "I know everybody!" And his thoughts went from one to another of the many people he knew; indeed, he knew everybody. "It is from my wife!" he said at last. "She's playing a trick on me! Charmant!"

But she wasn't playing a trick on him; that time was past.

Once more there was a party, but this one wasn't at the General's. It was a fancy-dress ball given by one of the princes; many of the guests wore masks.

The General went as Rubens, in a Spanish costume with a small ruff and a rapier, and carried himself well indeed. His wife was Madame Rubens, in black velvet with a high bodice that was terribly warm, and her neck in a millstone—that is to say, of course, a large ruff. She looked exactly like a Dutch painting of the General's, in which the hands were especially admired; they were an exact likeness of those of the General's wife. Emilie went as Psyche, in lace and muslin. She was a floating tuft of swansdown; she had no need of the wings and just wore them to show she was Psyche.

It was a scene of magnificent pomp and splendor, with lights and flowers and many riches, and all in good taste. There was so much to see that one hardly had a chance to take notice of Madame Rubens' beautiful hands.

Then a black domino, with an acacia flower in his hood, danced by with Psyche.

"Who's that?" asked the General's wife.

"His Royal Highness," said the General. "I'm quite sure of it. I knew him immediately by his handshake."

The Generals' wife was doubtful.

General Rubens wasn't doubtful. He drew the black domino aside and traced the royal initials in the palm of his hand.

They were denied, but a hint was given—the motto of the saddle—"One whom the General does not know!"

"But then I do know you!" said the General. "It was you who sent me the saddle." The domino waved his hand and disappeared among the dancers.

"Who was that black domino you were dancing with, Emilie?" asked the General's wife.

"I didn't ask his name," she replied.

"Because you knew it! It's the Professor! Count," she continued, turning to the Count, who stood nearby, "your protégé is here; the black domino with the acacia flower."

"It's quite possible, your ladyship," he replied. "But still, one of the princes is wearing the same costume."

"I know that handshake," said the General. "I received the saddle from the prince! I'm so sure I'm right that I am going to ask him to dinner."

"Do so," said the Count. "If it's the prince, he'll be sure to come."

"And if it's the other he won't come," said the General, making his way to the black domino, who was standing talking to the king. The General offered a most respectful invitation, together with hopes of a better acquaintance. He smiled confidently, for he knew quite well whom he was inviting, and he spoke loudly and distinctly.

The domino lifted his mask, and it was George!

"Does the General repeat his invitation?" he asked.

The General drew himself up an inch, took on a stiffer bearing, took two steps backward and one step forward, as if he were dancing a minuet. All the gravity and sternness he could muster—in short, all the General—were in his patrician features.

"I never go back on my word—the Professor is invited!" And he bowed, with a sidelong glance at the king, who must certainly have heard everything.

And so the General gave a dinner, and his only guests were the old count and his protégé.

"Now that I've got my foot under the table," thought George, "the foundation stone is laid."

And indeed it was; it was laid with great solemnity by the General and his wife.

The young man had come and gone and as the General well knew, had spoken like a member of good society and been most interesting; the General had even found himself repeating his "Charmant!" many times. The General's wife spoke of her dinner, spoke of it to one of the highest and most important of the court ladies, and the latter asked for an invitation for herself the next time the Professor should come. So of course, he had to be invited again. And invited he was, and came, and again he was "Charmant." He could even play chess!

"He doesn't come from the cellar," said the General. "Most certainly he is some scion of nobility; there are many such, and it isn't any fault of his!"

The Professor could enter the King's house, so he could very well enter the General's; but as for taking root there—there was no talk of that—except by the whole town!

He did take root, and he grew. The dew of grace had fallen from above.

So no one was surprised that, when the Professor became State Councillor, Emilie became Madame State Councillor.

"Life is either tragedy or comedy," said the General. "In a

tragedy people die; in a comedy they win each other."

And here they won each other. And they had three sturdy sons, though not all at once.

Whenever the sweet children came to see Grandfather or Grandmother, they galloped on sticks through rooms and halls. And the General rode on a stick behind them—"As a groom for the little State Councillors!" The General's wife sat on a sofa and smiled, even if she did have one of her bad headaches.

That's how far George got on in the world, and he got much farther, too; or else it wouldn't have been worth my while to tell you the story of "The Porter's Son."

THE TOAD
(1866)

The well was deep, and therefore the rope was long; the wheel went around with difficulty when the water-filled bucket had to be pulled up over the side of the well. The sun could never mirror itself down in the water, no matter how brightly it shone; but as far down as its rays penetrated, green weeds were growing from between the stones.

There was a family of toads living down there. It was an immigrant family which, as a matter of fact, had come down there headlong in the person of the old toad mother, who was still living. The green frogs that swam in the water had made their homes there for a much longer time, but they acknowledged their cousins and called them "well guests." The latter, however, had no thoughts of ever leaving; they found it very comfortable here on the dry land, as they called the wet stones.

Mamma Frog had once traveled; she'd been in the bucket when it had gone up, but the light above had been too strong for her and given her a frightful pain in the eyes. Luckily she had managed to get out of the bucket. She'd fallen into the water with a tremendous splash and been laid up for three days with a backache. She didn't have much to tell about the world above, but she did know, and so did all the others, that the well wasn't the whole world. Mamma Toad, on the other hand, might have told them a few things about it, but she never answered when anyone inquired, so they stopped inquiring.

"Big and ugly, fat and loathsome, she is!" said the young

green frogs. "And her brats are getting to be just like her!"

"Maybe so," said Mamma Toad, "but one of them has a jewel in its head, if I don't have it myself!"

And the green frogs listened and stared at her, and as they didn't like this news, they made faces at her and dived down to the bottom. But the young toads stretched out their hind legs proudly. Each of them thought it was the one which had the jewel, so they all kept their heads quite rigid, but at last they began to ask what it was they had to be proud of and just what a jewel was, anyway.

"It's something so glorious and precious," said Mamma Toad, "that I can't describe it. It's something you wear for your own pleasure and others become irritated over. But ask no more, for I won't answer."

"Well, I haven't got the jewel," said the smallest Toad, which was as ugly as it could be. "Why should I have anything so splendid? And if it irritates others, why, it wouldn't please me. No, all I want is to get up to the top of the well sometime and take one peep out! It must be wonderful up there!"

"Better stay where you are," said the old Toad. "You're at home here, and you know what it's like. Keep away from the bucket, or it may squash you! And even if you did get safely into it you might fall out. Not everyone can come down as luckily as I did and keep limbs and eggs all safe and sound."

"Croak!" said the little one; and that was the same as when we humans say, "Oh!"

It had such a great desire to get up to the top of the well and look out; it felt an intense longing for the green things up there. And next morning, when the bucket, filled with water, was being pulled up and happened to pause for an instant beside the stone where the Toad sat, the little creature quivered through and through and then jumped into the bucket. It sank to the bottom of the water, which soon was drawn up and emptied out.

"Phooie, what a nuisance!" said the man when he saw it. "That's the ugliest thing I've ever seen!" And then he kicked with his heavy wooden shoe at the Toad, which came close to being crippled, but managed to escape into the middle of some tall nettles. It saw stalk after stalk around it; it looked upward and saw the sun shining on the leaves, making them quite transparent.

For the Toad it was the same as it is for us when we come suddenly into a great forest, where the sun shines between leaves and branches.

"It's much prettier here than down in that well! You could stay here for your whole lifetime!" said the little Toad. It lay there for an hour; it lay there for two hours. "Now what could there be outside? Since I've come this far I might as well go farther." So it crept as fast as it could, until it came out into the road, where the sun shone on it; and then it was powdered with dust as it hopped across the road.

"Here one is really on dry land," said the Toad. "I'm getting almost too much of a good thing; it tickles right through me!"

Now it reached a ditch, where grew forget-me-nots and meadowsweet, while beyond it was a hedge of white thorn and elder bushes, with convolvulus creeping and hanging about it. What vivid colors there were to see here! And here flew a butterfly, too. The Toad thought it was a flower that had torn itself loose in order to get a better look at the world; that, of course, was very reasonable.

"If I could only move about like that!" said the Toad. "Croak! Oh! How glorious!" For eight days and nights, it remained by the ditch and felt no want of food. Then on the ninth day it thought, "Oh, forward." But was there anything more beautiful to be found anywhere? Perhaps a little toad or some green frogs; there had been a sound in the wind the night before which had seemed to indicate there were cousins in the neighborhood.

"It's wonderful to be alive! To come up out of that well and lie in the bed of nettles, to creep along and hop across the dusty road and rest in the wet ditch! But on, further forward! I must find frogs or a little toad; one can't do without companions, after all. Nature alone isn't enough for one!" And so it started its wanderings again.

In a field, it came to a large pond with rushes around it, and it went exploring in there.

"It's too wet for you in here, isn't it?" said the frog inside. "But you're quite welcome. Are you a he or a she? Not that it matters; you're equally welcome in either case."

And so it was invited to a concert that evening, a family concert, with a lot of gaiety and feeble voices; we all know that sort of affair. There were no refreshments, except free drinks—the whole pond, if they could drink it.

"Now I'll be traveling on," said the little Toad, which was always craving for something better.

It saw the stars twinkling, so large and so clear; it saw the new moon shine, and it saw the sun rise higher and higher.

"I think I'm still in a well, but a bigger well. I must get higher up! I feel a restlessness, a longing!" And when the moon was full and round, the poor creature thought, "I wonder if that is the bucket that's let down, and which I must hop into if I want to get higher? Or is the sun the big bucket? How large that is, and how bright! Why, it could hold all of us at once! I must watch for my chance! What a brightness there is in my head! I don't believe the jewel could shine more brightly. But I don't have the jewel, and I shall not cry for it. No; still higher in brightness and happiness! I feel confidence and yet fear. It's a hard step to take, but I must take it. On, further forward! Right on down the road!"

Then it moved along in leaps, as indeed such a creature can, until it reached the highway where humans lived. Here were both flower gardens and vegetable gardens. It stopped to rest by a cabbage garden.

"How many different beings there are that I've never known of! And how great and blessed the world is! But you must keep looking about you, instead of always sitting in the same place." And so it hopped into the cabbage garden. "How green it is here! How pretty it is here!"

"That I well know," said the Caterpillar on a cabbage leaf. "My leaf is the largest one here; it covers half the world, and the rest of the world I can do without!"

"Cluck! Cluck!" said somebody, and hens came hopping into the garden.

The first Hen was farsighted; she spied the worm on the curly leaf and pecked at it so that it fell to the ground, where it lay twisting and turning. The Hen looked at it first with one eye and then with the other, for she couldn't figure out what would become of that wriggling.

"It isn't doing that of its own accord," thought the Hen, and she raised her head to strike again. Whereupon the Toad became so frightened that it bumped right into the Hen.

"So that thing has auxiliary troops to fight for it!" she said. "Just look at that vermin!" Then the Hen turned away. "I don't care about that little green mouthful; it would only tickle my throat!" The other hens agreed with her, and so away they went.

"I got away from her with my wriggling," said the Caterpillar. "It's good to keep your presence of mind, but the hardest job is ahead—to get back up onto my cabbage leaf. Where is it?"

Then the little Toad came forward to sympathize. It was happy that its own ugliness had frightened away the Hen.

"What makes you think that?" asked the Caterpillar. "I wriggled away from her myself. You're indeed very unpleasant to look at! Let me get back to my own place. Now I can smell cabbage; I'm near my own leaf! There's nothing so beautiful as one's own. But I must get up higher."

"Yes, higher!" said the little Toad. "Higher up! It feels just as I do, but it isn't in a good humor today, because of its fright. We all want to get up higher!" And it looked up as high as it could.

A stork sat in his nest on the roof of the farmhouse; he clattered and the stork mother clattered.

"How high up they live!" thought the Toad. "If only I could get up there!"

In the farmhouse lived two young students; one was a poet, the other a naturalist. The one sang and wrote with gladness of all that God had created, as it was mirrored in his heart; he sang of it in short, clear, and rich, imposing verses. The other took hold of the creation itself, yes, and took it apart when it needed analyzing. He treated our Lord's work like a great piece of arithmetic; subtracted, multiplied, wanted to know it outside and inside, and to talk of it with intelligence, with complete understanding; and yet he talked of it with gladness and with wisdom. They were good, happy people, both of them.

"Why, there is a good specimen of a toad," said the Naturalist. "I must have it to preserve in alcohol!"

"You have two already," said the Poet. "Let it stay there in peace and enjoy itself."

"But it's so beautifully ugly!" said the other.

"If we could find the jewel in its head," said the Poet, "then I myself would give you a hand at splitting it open."

"The jewel!" said the other. "How well you know your natural history!"

"But isn't there something very splendid about the old folk legend that the toad, the ugliest of creatures, often has hidden in its head the most precious of jewels? Isn't it much the same with people? Wasn't there a jewel like that hidden in Aesop, and Socrates, too?"

The Toad didn't hear any more and hadn't understood half of what it had heard. The two friends went on, and it escaped being preserved in alcohol.

"They were talking about that jewel, too," said the Toad. "It's good that I don't have it; otherwise I would have got into trouble."

Then there was a clattering on the farmer's roof. Father Stork was giving a lecture to his family, and they were all looking down askance at the two young men in the cabbage garden.

"A human being is the most conceited of creatures," said the

Stork.

"Hear how they go on jabbering, and yet they can't even make as much noise as a rattle! They crow over their eloquence, their language! A fine language that is! It becomes more unintelligible even to them with each day's journey. We can speak our language the whole world over, in Denmark or in Egypt. As for flying, they can't do that at all. They crawl along by means of an invention they call a railway, but there they often get their necks broken. I get the shivers in my bill when I think of it! The world can exist without people. We could well do without them. May we only have frogs and earthworms!"

"My, that was a powerful speech!" thought the little Toad. "What a great man he is, and how high he sits up there! I never saw anyone that high before. And how well he can swim!" it exclaimed, for just then the Stork soared off into the air on outstretched wings.

And then Mother Stork talked in the nest. She told about the land of Egypt and the water of the Nile, and of all the wonderful mud there was to be found in foreign countries; it sounded entirely new and charming to the little Toad.

"I must get to Egypt!" it said. "If only the Stork would take me along, or if one of its youngsters would, I would do the little one some favor in turn, on his wedding day. Yes, I'll get to Egypt, because I'm lucky! All the longing and yearning I feel is surely better than having a jewel in one's head."

And still it had the true jewel! That eternal longing and desire to go upward, ever upward, was the jewel, and it shone within the little Toad, shone with gladness, shone brightly.

At that very moment the Stork came. He had seen the Toad in the grass, and now he swooped down and, not very gently, siezed the little creature. His bill pinched, and the wind whistled; this was anything but comfortable. But still the Toad was going upward, and off to Egypt, it knew; therefore its eyes brightened until it seemed as if a spark shot out from them.

"Croak! Oh!"

The body was dead; the little Toad had been killed. But the spark from its eyes—what became of that?

The sunbeam caught it up and bore away the jewel from the head of the Toad. Where?

You should not ask the Naturalist; rather ask the Poet. He'll tell it to you as a fairy tale; and the Caterpillar will be in it, and the Stork family will have a part in it. Just think—the Caterpillar will be changed into a beautiful butterfly. The Stork family will fly over mountains and seas to faraway Africa and yet find the shortest way home again to the land of Denmark, to the same village, to the same roof! Yes, it's all almost too much like a fairy tale, and still it is true! You may well ask the Naturalist about that; he'll have to admit it; and yet you know it yourself, for you've witnessed it.

But the jewel in the head of the Toad? Look for it in the sun; look at it if you can. The brightness is too great. We have not yet eyes that can look directly at all the glories God has created, but someday we shall have them, and that will be the most beautiful fairy tale of all, for we ourselves shall have a part in it.

THE GOBLIN AND THE WOMAN (1867)

You know the Goblin, but do you know the Woman—the Gardener's wife? She was very well read and knew poems by heart; yes, and she could write them, too, easily, except that the rhymes—"clinchings," as she called them—gave her a little trouble. She had the gift of writing and the gift of speech; she could very well have been a parson or at least a parson's wife.

"Earth is beautiful in her Sunday gown," she said, and this thought she had expanded and set down in poetic form, with "clinchings," making a poem that was so long and lovely.

The Assistant Schoolmaster, Mr. Kisserup (not that his name matters at all), was her nephew, and on a visit to the Gardener's he heard the poem. It did him good, he said, a lot of good. "You have soul, Madam," he said.

"Stuff and nonsense!" said the Gardener. "Don't be putting such ideas in her head! Soul! A wife should be a body, a good, plain, decent body, and watch the pot, to keep the porridge from burning."

"I can take the burnt taste out of the porridge with a bit of charcoal," said the Woman. "And I can take the burnt taste out of you with a little kiss. You pretend you don't think of anything but cabbage and potatoes, but you love the flowers, too." Then she kissed him. "Flowers are the soul!"

"Mind your pot!" he said, as he went off to the garden. That was his pot, and he minded it.

But the Assistant Schoolmaster stayed on, talking to the

woman. Her lovely words, "Earth is beautiful," he made a whole sermon of, which was his habit.

"Earth is beautiful, and it shall be subject unto you! was said, and we became lords of the earth. One person rules with the mind, one with the body; one comes into the world like an exclamation mark of astonishment, another like a dash that denotes faltering thought, so that we pause and ask, why is he here? One man becomes a bishop, another just a poor assistant schoolmaster, but everything is for the best. Earth is beautiful and always in her Sunday gown. That was a thought-provoking poem, Madam, full of feeling and geography!"

"You have soul, Mr. Kisserup," said the Woman, "a great deal of soul, I assure you. After talking with you, one clearly understands oneself."

And so they talked on, equally well and beautifully. But out in the kitchen somebody else was talking, and that was the Goblin, the little gray-dressed Goblin with the red cap—you know the fellow. The Goblin was sitting in the kitchen, acting as pot watcher. He was talking, but nobody heard him except the big black Pussycat—"Cream Thief," the Woman called him.

The Goblin was mad at her because he had learned she didn't believe in his existence. Of course, she had never seen him, but with all her reading she ought to have realized he did exist and have paid him a little attention. On Christmas Eve she never thought of setting out so much as a spoonful of porridge for him, though all his ancestors had received that, and even from women who had no learning at all. Their porridge used to be so swimming with cream and butter that it made the Cat's mouth water to hear about it.

"She calls me just a notion!" said the Goblin. "And that's

more than I can understand. In fact, she simply denies me! I've listened to her saying so before, and again just now in there, where she's driveling to that boy whipper, that Assistant Schoolmaster. I say with Pop, 'Mind the pot!' That she doesn't do, so now I am going to make it boil over!"

And the Goblin blew on the fire till it burned and blazed up. "Surre-rurre-rup!" And the pot boiled over.

"And now I'm going to pick holes in Pop's socks," said the Goblin. "I'll unravel a large piece, both in toe and heel, so she'll have something to darn; that is, if she is not too busy writing poetry. Madam Poetess, please darn Pop's stocking!"

The Cat sneezed; he had caught a cold, though he always wore a fur coat.

"I've opened the door to the larder," said the Goblin. "There's boiled cream in there as thick as paste. If you won't have a lick, I will."

"If I am going to get all the blame and the whipping for it, anyway," said the Cat, "I'll lick my share of the cream."

"First a lick, then a kick!" said the Goblin. "But now I'm off to the Assistant Schoolmaster's room, where I'll hang his suspenders on the mirror, put his socks into the water pitcher, and make him think the punch was too strong and has his brain in a whirl. Last night I sat on the woodpile by the kennel. I have a lot of fun teasing the watchdog; I let my legs dangle in front of him. The dog couldn't reach them, no matter how hard he jumped; that made him mad, he barked and barked, and I dingled and dangled; we made a lot of noise! The Assistant Schoolmaster woke up and jumped out of bed three times, but he couldn't see me, though he was wearing his spectacles. He always sleeps with his spectacles on."

"Say mew when you hear the Woman coming," said the Cat. "I'm a little deaf. I don't feel well today."

"You have the licking sickness," said the Goblin. "Lick away; lick your sickness away. But be sure to wipe your whiskers, so the cream won't show on it. I'm off to do a little eavesdropping."

So the Goblin stood behind the door, and the door stood ajar. There was nobody in the parlor except the Woman and the Assistant Schoolmaster. They were discussing things which, as the Assistant Schoolmaster so nobly observed, ought to rank in every household above pots and pans—the Gifts of the Soul.

"Mr. Kisserup," said the Woman, "since we are discussing this subject, I'll show you something along that line which I've never yet shown to a living soul—least of all a man. They're my smaller poems; however, some of them are rather long. I have called them 'Clinchings by a Danneqvinde.' You see, I am very fond of old Danish words!"

"Yes, we should hold onto them," said the Assistant Schoolmaster. "We should root the German out of our language."

"That I am doing, too!" said the Woman. "You'll never hear me speak of Kleiner or Butterteig; no, I call them fatty cakes and paste leaves."

Then she took a writing book, in a light green cover, with two blotches of ink on it, from her drawer.

"There is much in this book that is serious," she said. "My mind tends toward the melancholy. Here is my 'The Sign in the Night,' 'My Evening Red,' and 'When I Got Klemmensen'—my husband; that one you may skip over, though it has thought and feeling. 'The Housewife's Duties' is the best one—sorrowful, like all the rest; that's my best style. Only one piece is comical; it contains some lively thoughts—one must indulge in them occasionally—thoughts about—now, you mustn't laugh at me—thoughts about being a poetess! Up to now it has been a secret between me and my drawer; now you know it, too, Mr. Kisserup. I love poetry; it haunts me; it jeers, advises, and commands. That's what I mean by my title, 'The Little Goblin.' You know the old peasants' superstitions about the Goblin who is always playing tricks in the house. I myself am the house, and my poetical feelings are the Goblin, the spirit that possesses me. I have written about his power and strength in 'The Little Goblin'; but you must promise with your hands and lips never to give away my secret, either to my husband or to anyone else. Read it loud, so that I can tell if you understand the meaning."

And the Assistant Schoolmaster read, and the Woman listened, and so did the little Goblin. He was eavesdropping, you'll remember, and he came just in time to hear the title 'The Little Goblin.'

"That's about me!" he said. "What could she have been written about me? Oh, I'll pinch her! I'll chip her eggs, and pinch her chickens, and chase the fat off her fatted calf! Just watch me do it!"

And then he listened with pursed lips and long ears; but when he heard of the Goblin's power and glory, and his rule over the woman (she meant poetry, you know, but the Goblin took the name literally), the little fellow began grinnning more and more. His eyes brightened with delight; then the corners of his mouth set sternly in lines of dignity; he drew himself up on his toes a whole inch higher than usual; he was greatly pleased with what was written about the Little Goblin.

"I've done her wrong! The Woman has soul and fine breeding! How, I have done her wrong! She has put me into her 'Clinchings,' and they'll be printed and read. Now I won't allow the Cat to drink her cream; I'll do that myself! One drinks less than two, so that'll be a saving; and that I shall do, and pay honor and respect to the Woman!"

"He's a man all right, that Goblin," said the old Cat. "Just one sweet mew from the Woman, a mew about himself, and he immediately changes his mind! She is a sly one, the Woman!"

But the Woman wasn't sly; it was just that the Goblin was a man.

If you can't understand this story, ask somebody to explain it to you; but don't ask the Goblin or the Woman, either.

THE DRYAD
(1868)

We're going to Paris to see the exposition!

Now we're there! It was a speedy journey, done completely without witchcraft—we went by steam, in a ship and on a railroad. Our time is indeed a time of fairy tales.

Now we are in a large hotel in the middle of Paris. The staircase is decorated with flowers, and soft carpets are spread over the steps. Our room is pleasant; the balcony door is open, and we can look out onto a large square. Down there is spring, which has come to Paris, having arrived at the same time we did, in the form of a big, young chestnut tree with delicate leaves beginning to open. How much more richly that tree is dressed in the beauty of spring than the other trees on the square! One of them has stepped out of the row of living trees and lies on the ground with its roots torn up. Where that tree stood the young chestnut will be planted, and there it will grow.

It is still standing high up on the heavy wagon that brought it to Paris this morning from many miles out in the country. For years it had stood out there, close to a mighty oak, under which the pious old pastor often used to sit and tell his stories to the listening children. Of course, the young chestnut tree had also listened.

The Dryad that lived in this tree was then but a child; she could remember way back when the chestnut tree was so small it could hardly peep over the tall grass blades and ferns. These were then as large as they ever would be; but the tree grew bigger every year, drinking in air and sunshine, dew and rain; the powerful winds shook it and bent it back and forth, which was an important part of its education.

The Dryad was pleased with her life and enjoyed living, was pleased with the sunshine and the songs of birds; but she liked best of all the human voice for she knew the language of people as well as that of the animals. Butterflies, cockchafers, and dragonflies—indeed, everything that could fly came to visit her, and everyone that came would gossip. They talked about the villages, the vineyards, the woods, and the old castle with its park, in which there were dikes and canals; down there in water also dwelt beings who in their own way could fly from place to place—beneath the water—beings with knowledge and imagination, but who said nothing, for they were too wise. The swallow, which often dived down deep into the water, told about the bright goldfish, the fat turbot, the sturdy perch, and the old moss-covered carp. The swallow gave very good descriptions, but it's always better to go and look for oneself, it said. But how could the Dryad ever see all these things? She had to be satisfied with the beautiful landscape and the buzz of human activity.

Everything was delightful, but most delightful when the old pastor stood there under the oak tree and talked about France and about the great deeds of men and women whose names are remembered through the ages with admiration. The Dryad heard of the shepherd maid, Joan of Arc, of Charlotte Corday; she learned of ancient times, and the times of Henry IV and Napoleon I, and she even heard of the genius and glory of our own times. She heard of names that were deep in the hearts of the people, and that France is the world's country, the world's gathering place of genius, with the cradle of liberty at its center.

The village children listened attentively, and the Dryad just as attentively; she became a schoolchild like the rest. In the shapes of the drifting clouds she could see many pictures of those things she had learned. The cloudy sky was her picture book.

She had thought she was very happy in this beautiful France, but she began to believe that the birds—in fact, all creatures that could fly—were much better off than she. Even the fly could look far beyond her horizon. France was so large and so beautiful, but she could see only a very small part of it. France was as broad as the world, with vineyards and forests and great cities, and of all these Paris was the greatest and most glorious! The birds could fly there, but she, never!

Among the village children there was a little girl so ragged and so poor, but very pretty to look upon. She was always singing and laughing, and often tied red flowers in her black hair.

"Don't go to Paris!" said the old pastor. "Poor child, if you go there it will be the ruin of you!"

And yet she went. The Dryad often thought of her, for they had both had the same desire and yearning to see the great city.

Spring came, and then summer; autumn came, and then winter. A couple of years went by.

The Dryad's tree was bearing its first chestnut blossoms, and the birds chirped around them in the bright sunlight. A noble lady came driving along the road in a grand carriage. She herself was driving the beautiful and spirited horses, with a smartly dressed little groom sitting behind her. The Dryad recognized her; the old pastor knew her. He shook his head and said sadly, "You did go there, and it proved your ruin, poor Marie!"

"She, poor?" thought the Dryad. "No! What a change! She's dressed like a duchess; that's what she got in the city of enchantment. Oh, if only I were there in all that light and splendor! When I look over there where I know the city is, I can see how it lights up the clouds in the night."

Indeed, she would look in that direction every evening, every night; there she could see the brightness along the horizon. On clear, moonlit nights she missed the bright cloudiness; she missed the drifting clouds that showed her pictures of the great city and its history.

The child clings to its picture book. The Dryad clings to her cloud book, her book of thoughts.

A balmy, cloudless sky was like a blank page to her, and it had now been several days since she had seen one like that. It was summertime, and the days were hot and sultry, without a cooling breeze; every flower and leaf was drowsy, and people were, too.

The clouds rose at that corner of the horizon where in the night the brightness announced, "Here is Paris!" All the clouds gathered and rose together, forming what appeared to be whole mountains; they pushed through the air and spread out over the entire countryside as far as the Dryad could see. They were heaped in mighty, rocklike, thundery-blue masses, layer on layer, high into the air. Then flashes of light shot out from them. "These are also the servants of God our Master," the old pastor had said. And then out flashed a bluish, blinding light, a blaze of lightning, which tried to rival the sun itself; it shattered the piled-up clouds.

The lightning struck down, down at the mighty old oak tree, splitting it to its very roots; the crown was shattered, the trunk torn apart. The tree crashed down and fell as if spreading itself out to receive the messenger of light. Not even the mightiest cannon could roar through the air and over the land at the birth of a king's son as did the thunder in saluting the passing of the old oak tree.

The rain streamed down. A refreshing breeze sprang up; the storm was over, and a holiday calm settled on the countryside. The villagers gathered around the fallen old oak tree; the old pastor spoke a few words in praise of it, and a painter made a sketch of the old tree as a lasting souvenir.

"Everything passes on," said the Dryad, "passes on as the clouds do, never to return."

Never again did the pastor come there. The roof of the schoolhouse had crashed in, and the pulpit was broken. No more did the children come. But autumn came, and winter came, and then spring. And during this time the Dryad's eyes were turned toward that corner on the distant horizon where every evening and night the lights of Paris shone like a belt of radiance. Out of Paris sped locomotive after locomotive, train after train, whistling and roaring, constantly. At every hour, in the evenings, at midnight, in the morning, and throughout the day, the trains arrived, and from these, and into these, people from all countries of the world pushed. A new wonder of the world drew them to Paris. How did this wonder show itself?

"A gorgeous flower of art and industry," people said, "has

sprung up on the barren sands of the Champ de Mars. It's a gigantic sunflower, and from its leaves you can study geography or statistics, or become as wise as a councilman, or be inspired by art and poetry, or learn about the products and greatness of every country.

"It's a fairy-tale flower," others said, "a colored lotus, spreading its green leaves like a velvet carpet, the leaves that shot up in the early spring. Summer will see it in its greatest glory, and the storms of autumn will blow it away, leaving neither leaves nor roots."

Before the military school, the Champ de Mars lay stretched out in time of peace, a field without grass and straw, a piece of sandy desert cut from the African wilderness, where Fata Morgana shows her mysterious air castles and hanging gardens; they were more magnificent, more wondrous, now on the Champ de Mars, for they had been converted into reality by human skill.

"They have built the palace of the modern Aladdin," it was said. "Day after day, hour after hour, it unfolds more and more of its new splendors."

There was an endless array of halls in marble and many colors. The giant with bloodless veins moved his steel and iron limbs there in the great circular hall. Works of art in metal, in stone, in tapestry, loudly proclaimed the powerful genius that labored in all the lands of the world. There were picture galleries and flower shows. Everything that hand and brain could create was on exhibition in the workshop of the mechanic. Even relics from ancient castles and peat moors were to be found there. The overwhelmingly great, colorful show should have been reproduced in miniature and squeezed into the dimensions of a toy, to be seen and appreciated in its entirety.

There on the Champ de Mars stood, as on a huge Christmas table, Aladdin's castle of art and industry, and around it were knickknacks of greatness from every country; every nation found a memory of its home.

There was the royal palace of Egypt, and there a caravansery from the desert. The Bedouin from the land of the hot sun galloped past; and there were the Russian stables, with beautiful fiery horses from the steppes. Over there was the small thatched cottage of a Danish peasant, with Dannebrog, the flag of Denmark, next to Gustavus Vasa's beautifully carved wooden cottage from Dalarne. American log cabins, English cottages, French pavilions, mosques, churches, and theaters were all spread about in a wonderful manner. And in the middle of all this was the fresh green turf, with clear running water, flowering shrubs, rare trees, and glass houses where one might imagine oneself in a tropical forest. Complete rose gardens, brought from Damascus, bloomed in glory under glass roofs. What colors and fragrance! Artificial grottoes contained specimens of various fishes in fresh- and salt-water ponds—it was like standing at the bottom of the ocean there among the fishes and polyps.

Word spread that all these things were now being exhibited on the Champ de Mars, and an immense crowd of human beings crawled all over this richly decked feast table like a swarm of ants on a journey. Some went on foot or were drawn in wagons, for not everyone's legs can endure such tiresome traveling.

From early dawn until late at night they came there. Steamer after steamer, crowded with visitors, glided down the Seine.

The mass of carriages was continually increasing, and the multitude of travelers on foot and horseback increased; streetcars and busses were jammed, packed, and spilling over with human beings. All these currents flowed toward one goal—the Paris Exposition!

Every entrance was bright with the flag of France, and around the bazaar of all nations waved the flags of the various countries. A burring and buzzing sounded from the hall of the machines, and chimes rang out from the towers, while the tones of the organs sounded from the churches, mingled with hoarse, nasal strains from Oriental coffeehouses. It was a Babel empire, a Babel language, a wonder of the world.

All this really happened—at least, according to reports. Who hasn't heard about it? The Dryad knew all about it; she knew everything that has been told here of the world's new wonder in the city of cities. "Hurry, all you birds, fly there and see it; then come back and tell me about it!" was the prayer of the Dryad.

Her longing grew until it became a great desire; it became the one thought of her life. And then...

In the silent, solemn night the full moon was shining, and from its face the Dryad saw a spark come forth, as bright as a falling star, and fall to the foot of the tree, whose branches shivered as if shaken by a tempest—and then a mighty, shining figure stood there. It spoke with a tender voice, and yet as powerfully as the judgment-day trumpet that kisses to life and calls to judgment.

"You shall go to the city of enchantments! There you shall take root and enjoy the air and the sunshine, but your life shall be shortened. The long procession of years that awaited you here in the open country will shrink to a small number. Poor Dryad, it will be your ruin! Your longing will grow and your great desire and craving will increase until the tree itself will be a prison to you. You will leave your shelter and change your nature; you will fly forth to mingle with human beings, and then your years will shrink to half of a mayfly's lifetime—to one night only! The flame of your life will be blown out. The leaves of the tree will wither and blow away, never to return."

So said the voice; thus it rang out. And then the shining being disappeared—but not the Dryad's longing and desire; she trembled in a violent fever of anticipated joy. Rejoicingly she said, "I shall go the city of cities. Life will begin for me—floating like the clouds, whither no one knows!"

The time of fulfillment came at early dawn, when the moon had grown pale and the skies had reddened; then the words of promise were to come true. Men came with spades and poles. They dug carefully around and deep under the roots of the tree. Then they lifted the tree out of the ground with its roots and the earth about them, and wound straw mats around the roots to make a warm foot bag. And then the tree was set on a wagon and tied securely. Now it was to go on a journey to Paris, and it was to remain and grow in the great metropolis of France, the city of cities.

The branches and leaves of the chestnut tree trembled as they began to move it. The Dryad trembled, too, but with the joy of expectation.

"Away! Away!" sounded every heartbeat. "Away! Away!" rang the trembling words of longing. The Dryad forgot to say "Farewell" to her old home, to the swaying blades of grass and the innocent daisies that had looked up to her as to a great lady in the garden of our Father, a young princess playing shepherdess in the country.

The chestnut tree on the wagon nodded "Farewell" or "Away!"—the Dryad didn't know which. Her thoughts and dreams were of the wonderful new and yet familiar life which would soon unfold itself. Neither the happy heart of an innocent child nor the heart filled with passion was ever more filled with thought than hers was on her journey to Paris.

Not "Farewell!"—but "Away! Away!" The wagon wheels turned round and round; the distance came near and then soon lay behind. The country changed, as the clouds above changed. New vineyards, woods, villages, villas, and gardens came into view, came closer, and then rolled past. The chestnut tree moved on, and the Dryad moved on with it. Locomotive after locomotive roared past. They blew clouds that took on the shapes of figures, which spoke of Paris, where they came from and where the Dryad was going.

Of course, everything around her knew where she was going. It seemed to her that every tree she passed stretched its branches toward her and begged, "Take me with you! Take me with you!" In every tree there lived a yearning dryad.

What a change! What a trip! The houses seemed to come springing right up out of the ground, more and more of them, closer and closer together. Chimneys appeared like flowerpots, placed side by side, one after another, on the roofs. Huge inscriptions, in letters a yard long, and colorfully painted figures covered the walls from ground to roofs, and shone brightly.

"Where does Paris begin, and when will I be there?" the Dryad asked herself.

There were increasing crowds of people; the tumult and

noise grew louder. Carriage followed carriage; people were on foot and on horseback. There were shops on all sides, and music, song, talking, and screaming.

Now the Dryad, in her tree, was in the center of Paris.

The big, heavy wagon stopped in a little square where trees were planted and around which were high houses. Every window had its own balcony, and from these people looked down at that fresh, young chestnut tree which had been driven there to be planted in the place of the dead, uprooted tree that lay on the ground. People passing by stopped for a while to smile at that fresh green bit of early spring. The older trees, their leaves yet scarcely budding, greeted it with rustling branches: "Welcome! Welcome!" And the fountain, which spouted its water into the air so that it splashed into the basin, let the wind carry a few drops to the new arrival, to give it welcome drink.

The Dryad felt the tree being taken down from the wagon and then being put into its destined home. The roots were covered with earth, and fresh green turf was laid on top of that. Blooming shrubs were planted, and earthen pots with flowers in them were placed about. Thus a whole little garden appeared in the midst of the square.

The dead, uprooted tree, killed by gas fumes, hearth smoke, and all the stifling city air, was thrown upon the wagon and hauled away. The crowd watched; old people and children sat upon the bench in the little park, looking at the leaves of the newly planted tree. And we, who tell you about all this, stood on our balcony, gazing down on the young tree that had just come from the fresh air of the country and said what the old pastor would have said if he had been there: "Poor Dryad!"

"How happy I am, how happy!" said the Dryad. "And yet I can't quite understand it. I can't explain how I feel; it all seems to be the way I thought it would be, and yet it isn't quite what I expected!"

The houses were so high and so close. The sun shone upon only one wall; that was covered with posters and placards, and people crowded and thronged around it. Carriages rushed by, light ones and heavy ones. Busses, filled to overflowing, rattled by like moving houses. Carts and carriages squabbled over the right of way.

"Won't these overgrown houses standing so stiflingly close," thought the Dryad, "move away and make room for other shapes and forms, the way the clouds do in the sky? Why don't they move aside, so I can really see Paris and beyond Paris?" She felt she had to see Notre-Dame, the Vendôme Column, and the many wonderful works that had drawn and were still drawing so many people there.

But the houses didn't move from their places.

The lamps were lighted while it was still daylight, and the gaslight gleamed from all the shopwindows, lighting up the branches of the trees; it was almost like summer sunlight. But the stars above looked exactly the same as the Dryad had seen them back home. She thought she felt a clean and mild breeze come from there. She felt uplifted, strengthened, and could feel a new vigor flow through the tree from the very tips of the leaves to its roots. She then realized that she was in the world of living people and felt she was looked upon with kindly eyes; all around her were tumult and tones, colors and lights. The tones of wind instruments came to her from the side streets, hurdy-gurdies playing dance-provoking melodies. Yes, for dancing, for dancing! For pleasure and amusement, these were played. It was a music to make men and horses, even carriages trees, and houses, dance, if they could. All this fanned an intoxicating yearning for pleasure in the heart of the Dryad.

"How glorious! How beautiful all this is!" she cried rejoicingly. "I'm in Paris!"

The day that came, and the night that followed it, and then the following day brought the same display, the same uproar, the same life, changing and yet always the same.

"By now I know every tree and flower in this square; I know every house, balcony, and shop in this little corner where they've stuck me and where I can see nothing of the great and mighty city. Where is the Arc de Triomphe, and the boulevards, and that wonder of the world? I can't see anything of all this. I stand as if imprisoned in a cage here among these high houses, which I know by heart now, with all their inscriptions, posters, and placards—all the painted delicacies for which I have no more appetite. Where is that which I've heard so much about, which I have known and longed for, the reason I wanted to come here? What have I got—gained, found? I yearn as much as I did before. I know the life I want. I want to go out among the living people and mingle with them; I want to fly like the birds and see and feel and become like a human being! I would rather really live for half a day than spend a lifetime of years in daily idleness and languor, becoming sick, sinking, falling like dew in the meadow, and then disappearing! I want to sail like the clouds, bathe in the sun of life, look down on everything below as the clouds do, and then disappear as they do—where, no one knows!"

This was the sigh of the Dryad, going aloft as a prayer.

"Take from me all my years of life and grant me but half of a mayfly's life! Free me from my prison; give me human life and human happiness, though it be but for a fleeting moment, for only this one night, and then punish me, if you wish, for my longing for life! Free me, even if this dwelling of mine, this fresh young tree, wither, be cut down, turned to ashes, and blown away by the winds!"

There was a rustling among the boughs of the tree, and a strange sensation came over it. Every leaf shivered, and fiery sparks seemed to shoot forth from them. A gust of wind shook the crown of the tree. And then there came forth a feminine form—the Dryad herself! In the same instant she found herself beneath the green boughs, rich with leaves and lit by gaslight from all sides. She was as young and beautiful as poor Marie, to whom one had said, "The great city will be your ruin!"

The Dryad sat at the foot of the tree, which she had locked and whose key she had thrown away. So young, so lovely! The stars saw her, and they twinkled; the gas lamps saw her as they glittered, beckoning to her. How slender she was, and yet so strong, a child and yet a full-grown maiden! Her dress was as smooth as silk, as green as the freshly unfolded leaves of the crown of the tree. In her nut-brown hair was a half-opened chestnut blossom. She looked like the Goddess of Spring.

For a brief moment she sat there motionless, and then she bounded off around the corner like a gazelle. She ran and darted the way reflected sunbeams dart here and there from a mirror being moved in the sunshine. If one had looked closely and could have seen what was there to see, how wondrous this would have been to him! Whenever she rested a moment, the color of her dress and of her figure was changed, according to the nature of the place where she stood and the lights that fell on her.

She reached the boulevards, where there was an ocean of light from the gas flames in the street lamps, stores, and cafés. There were rows of young and slender trees, each of which shielded its dryad from the artificial sunlight. The whole vast sidewalk was like one large dining room, with tables of all sorts of refreshments, from champagne and chartreuse to coffee and beer. There were exhibits of flowers, pictures, statues, books, and colored materials.

From the crowd by the high houses she watched the roaring streams between the rows of trees; there was a surging river of rolling wagons, cabriolets, chariots, busses, coaches, men on horseback, and marching troops. Life and limb were endangered by any attempt to cross to the other side. Now a blue light shone the brightest, and then the gaslight was again the most brilliant; a rocket had suddenly shot up—from where, to where?

Surely this must be the greatest highway of the world's greatest city! There were charming Italian melodies and Spanish songs with castanet accompaniment. But the strains from Minutet's music box drowned all the other sounds—that exciting cancan music which Orpheus never knew and Helen never heard. Even the wheelbarrow would have danced on its one wheel if it could have. The Dryad did dance; she whirled and soared, and changed colors like a hummingbird in the sunshine, every house and its interior being reflected on her.

As the glorious lotus flower, torn from its roots, is carried away by the whirling river, so was the Dryad carried along, and whenever she stopped she changed into a new form; consequently, no one could follow her, recognize her, or even view her. Everything passed by her like cloud pictures—face after face—but she recognized none of them; she saw no familiar forms from home. Before her mind came two bright eyes, and she thought at once of Marie. Poor Marie, that ragged, gay child with the red flowers in her black hair. She was here in this worldly city—rich and charming, as when she had driven by the pastor's house, the Dryad's tree and the old oak. More than likely, she was somewhere in this deafening uproar; perhaps she had just alighted from that magnificent carriage waiting over there. Brilliant carriages, with richly liveried coachmen and footmen wearing silk stockings, were drawn up in a line, and the nobility alighting from them were all ladies, beautifully dressed. They passed through the open gates and ascended the broad, high steps that led into that stately building with the marble columns. Could this, perhaps, be the great wonder of the world? Surely Marie must be there!

"Sancta Maria!" was being sung within. The fragrance of incense rolled out under the high, painted and gilded arch, where it was always twilight. This was the Church of the Madeleine.

Dressed in the most costly black, fashioned after the finest and newest modes, the ladies of the aristocracy glided over the polished floor. Crests sparkled from the clasps of magnificent prayerbooks bound in velvet and were embroidered on perfumed handkerchiefs bordered with costly Brussels lace. A few of the women knelt in silent prayer before the high altar; others went to the confessionals. The Dryad felt an uneasiness, a fear, as if she were in a place where she should not be. It was a house of silence, a great hall of mystery and secrecy. Everything was said in whispers or in silent trust.

Now the Dryad realized that she was wrapped in silk and a lace veil, like the ladies of wealth and noble birth. Was every one of them a child of desire and longing like herself?

A deep, painful sigh was heard; did it come from the confessional or from the bosom of the Dryad? She drew the veil more closely about her. She was breathing in incense fumes and not the fresh air. This was not the place she had long for.

"Away, away! Take flight, without rest! The mayfly that lives but a day has no rest; her flight is her life!"

The Dryad was out again among the bright gas lamps and the magnificent fountains. "Not all the water from the fountain can wash away the blood of the innocents slain here!"

Those words were spoken. Here stood many strangers who spoke in loud and lively tones, which no one had dared to do in the great hall of secrecy from which she had just come.

A big stone slab was turned and then raised—why, she did not understand. She saw an opening into the depths of Earth. The strangers stepped down, leaving the starlit sky, the brilliant gaslights, and all the life of the living.

"I'm afraid!" said one of the women who stood here. "I don't dare go down! I care little about seeing the wonders there. Stay here with me!"

"And go home?" said a man. "Leave Paris without having seen the most remarkable thing of all, the wonderwork of modern times, the result of one man's mind and skill?"

"I'll not go down there," was the reply.

"The wonderwork of modern times," it had been said. And the Dryad had heard this and understood. At last she was to reach the goal of her greatest longing, and here was the entrance—down to the vast depths beneath Paris. She had not expected this, but now she had heard about it and had seen the strangers descend, and she followed them.

The steps were of cast iron, spiral-shaped, broad and comfortable; a lamp was burning below, and deeper down there was another. She found herself in a labyrinth of endless passages and halls crossing each other. Every street and lane in Paris could be seen there, as if reflected in a mirror. Their names could be read, and every house above had its number here, and its root, which led down under the hard, lonely walk that squeezed its way along the wide canal with its onward-rolling drainage. Above this was the aqueduct of fresh running water, and still higher gas pipes and telegraph wire hung like a network. Lamps shone in the distance, as if they were reflected images from the worldly city above. Now and then a rumbling could be heard overhead; it came from the heavy wagons crossing the bridges. Where was the Dryad?

You have heard of the catacombs; they are nothing compared with this underground world, this wonder of our times, the sewers of Paris! That was where the Dryad was, and not at the World's Fair on the Champ de Mars.

On all sides were heard exclamations of astonishment, wonder, and approval.

"Out of the deep here," they said, "come health and long life for the thousands above. Our age is the age of progress, with all its blessings!"

That was the opinion of people, the talk of people, but not that of the scavengers who were born here and built their homes and lived here—the rats. From the cracks of an old stone wall the rats squeaked so loudly and distinctly that the

Dryad could understand them. A big, old rat whose tail had been bitten off piped in a shrill voice of his feelings, his anguish, and the only idea in his mind; and his whole family approved of every word he said.

"I am disgusted by the meow, the human meow, the ignorant talk! Indeed, everything is very fine now, with gas and oil, but I don't eat such things. It has become so clean and light here that one is ashamed and doesn't know what one is ashamed of. I wish we lived in the good old days of the tallow candles; those times are not so far back—those romantic times, as people call them."

"What are you talking about?" asked the Dryad. "I've never seen you before. What are you talking about?"

"The wonderful old days," said the rat, "the days when Great-grandfather and Great-grandmother rat were young. At that time it was a great adventure to come down here. Those were the days for the rats of Paris! Mother Pest used to live down here then; she would kill human beings, but never rats. Robbers and smugglers could breathe freely down here. Then this was the asylum for the most fascinating characters I ever saw, such characters as one sees nowadays only in the melodramatic plays. Those romantic days have gone, even for us rats; we have fresh air now—and petroleum!"

Thus the rat squeaked, squeaked over the new times, and in honor of the good old days with Mother Pest.

Now they came to a carriage, a sort of open bus, drawn by two small, lively ponies. The group entered and drove along the Boulevard Sébastopol—that is, along the underground boulevard. Right above them, in Paris, was the real boulevard of that name, crowded with people.

The carriage disappeared in the twilight, and the Dryad disappeared, too, but she came to light again in the fresh, open air under the glare of the gas lamps. Here the wonder was to be found, and not in the damp atmosphere of the crossing and recrossing passages. Here she found the wonder of the world, which she had been seeking in her short lifetime. It burst forth in far richer glory than all the gaslights above, stronger than the Moon, which was now gliding by.

Yes, indeed, she saw it greet her; it winked and twinkled like Venus in the heavens. She saw a brilliant gate open into a little garden gay with light and dance music. Colored gas lamps shone on small artificial lakes and ponds, where water plants, artistically made of bent and painted tinsel, were displayed, and these hurled jets of water high into the air from their chalices, the water sparkling under the brilliant lights. Graceful weeping willows—real, spring weeping willows—trailed their fresh green branches in curving waves, like a transparent and yet screening veil. A bowl of light among the shrubbery threw its red glow over half-lit bowers made of green foliage, while magic tones of music thrilled the ears, teasing and alluring and chasing the blood through the human limbs.

She saw beautiful young women in evening dress, with innocent smiles on their lips, and laughing with the carelessness of youth. There was a Marie with roses in her hair, but with no carriage or footmen. How they whirled about; how they swung in that wild dance, now up, now down! They laughed and smiled, and leaped as if smitten by the tarantella dance; they looked so joyous, so gay, as if ready to embrace the whole world through pure happiness!

The Dryad felt herself irresistibly drawn into the dance. Her small, delicate feet were shod in silken shoes as brown as the ribbon that fluttered from her hair onto her bare shoulders. The large folds of the green silk dress enveloped her, but could not hide the perfectly shaped legs and the dainty feet, which seemed to be trying to draw a magic circle in the air before her dancing cavalier's head. Was she in the enchanted garden of Armida? What was the name of this place? In bright gas flames outside shone the name "Mabille."

There were shouts and applause, rockets and running water, and the popping of champagne bottles. The dance was bacchanalian, wild. And above all this the Moon was sailing across the sky, its face sloping a bit. The sky was cloudless, clear and pure, and one thought of looking right into Heaven from Mabille.

A consuming intoxication seized the Dryad, like the aftereffect of opium. Her eyes spoke, and her lips spoke, but her words were drowned by the tones of flute and violin. Her cavalier whispered words in her ear with the rhythm of the cancan; she did not understand them, nor do we understand them. He stretched his arms out to her, around her—but embraced only the transparent, gas filled air! The Dryad was carried away by the wind like a rose petal; and high in the air she saw a flame ahead, a brilliant light at the top of a tower. This light came from the goal of her desires, from the red lighthouse of the Fata Morgana of the Champ de Mars. The spring breeze carried her to it. She circled around the tower, and the workmen thought it was a butterfly that had come too early in the spring and was fluttering down to die.

The Moon was shining, and so were the gaslights and lanterns in the great halls, and throughout the widespread buildings of all nations they shone on the green hills and on the rocks that human skill had created and over which waterfalls were precipitated by the power of the "bloodless giant."

The depths of the oceans and of bodies of fresh water—the realm of fishes—were displayed there. One could imagine oneself at the bottom of the sea—deep down in a diving bell, with the water pressing hard on all sides against the thick glass walls. Fathom-long polyps, flexible, bending like eels, trembling with living thorns, swayed to and fro and held fast to the bottom of the sea.

A large flounder lay close by in deep thought, spreading himself out comfortably. A crab, resembling an enormous spider, crawled over him, while the shrimps moved about swiftly and restlessly, as if they were the moths and butterflies of the ocean.

Many beautiful plants were growing in the fresh water. Goldfish had arranged themselves in rows like red cows in a pasture, with all their heads in one direction, so that the stream would flow into their mouths. Thick, fat tenches stared with dull eyes at the glass walls; they knew they were in the Paris Exposition; they knew they had completed a tiring journey in tubs filled with water, and had been on a railroad train, where they had become landsick as men become seasick on the ocean. They had also come to see the Exposition, and they saw it from their own salt- or freshwater "loges," gazing at the swarms of humans that passed by from morning to night. All the countries of the world had sent their specimens of humanity there, so that the old tenches and breams, the perch and moss-covered carps, might look at the creatures and give their opinions about the various tribes.

"Man is a scalefish," said a slimy little carp, "changing his scales two or three times a day. They make mouth noises—speaking, they call it. We don't change our scales, and we make ourselves understood much more easily, by the motions of the corners of our mouths and the look in our eyes. We have many advantages over men."

"But they've learned how to swim," said a small freshwater fish. "I come from the great inland lake, and in the hot days of summer people go into the water there, but first they strip off their scales and then they swim. The frogs have taught them how to do it; the hind legs push and the front legs row, but they can't do it very long. They think they can rival us, but they can't. Poor people!"

The fishes stared; they thought that the crowd of people there now was the same one they had seen in the bright daylight; yes, and they even believed those figures were the same ones that had beaten against their nerves of observation on the very first day.

A little perch with pretty, mottled skin and an enviably rounded back said he was sure that the same "human scum" was still there.

"I can see it, too, very plainly," said a golden tench. "I distinctly see a beautiful, well-shaped human, a 'long-legged lady,' or whatever it is they call her. She has mouth corners and staring eyes like us, two balloons in the back, a folded umbrella hanging down in front, and a lot of seaweed on her dingling and dangling. She ought to throw all that off and go about the way we do, in nature's gift, and then she would look like an honorable tench—that is, as much as a human can look like us."

"What's become of that laced one, that he-human?"

"He was riding around here in a wheel chair, sitting there with paper, ink, and a pen, and writing everything down. What was he doing? They called him a journalist."

"He is still riding around!" said a moss-covered, old-maid carp who had a bit of worldly temptation stuck in her throat, making her quite hoarse. She had once swallowed a fishhook and since then had been swimming about tolerantly with the hook in her throat. "Journalist," she said; "that's spoken like a fish. It really means a sort of octopus among men!"

Thus the fishes talked on in their own way. But amid this artificial grotto and its water-filled tanks there sounded hammer blows and the songs of workmen, who had to work at night in order to get everything completed. These songs resounded in the midsummer night's dream of the Dryad, who stood there herself, but was soon to fly again and disappear.

"These are goldfish," she said, and nodded to them. "I'm glad to have been able to see you. Yes, I know you and have known you for a long time! The swallow told me all about you in my own home. How pretty and shining and charming you are! I could kiss each and every one of you! I know the others, too. That must be a crucian, and this is a delicate bream, and there's an old moss-covered carp. I know you, but you don't know me."

The fishes just stared, unable to understand a word she said; they gazed through the dim twilight.

The Dryad was gone; she was in the open air again, where the world's "wonder flower" spread its fragrance from many lands—from the rye-bread land, the codfish seashore, the Russian-leather country, eau-de-cologne valley, and rose-oil

Orient.

When we drive home half asleep in our carriage after a ball, the melodies we have heard continue to ring plainly in our ears, and we may sing each of them again. And as in the dead man's eye the last impression received in life remains photographed for some time, so the impression of the day's tumult and brilliance remained yet upon the eye of the night; it was neither absorbed nor quite blown away. The Dryad could see it and knew that it would persist even into the morrow.

Now the Dryad was among fragrant roses; she thought she recognized them as being from her own country, from the castle park and the garden of the pastor. She also saw a red pomegranate blossom; it was one like this that Marie had worn in her coal-black hair. The memory of her childhood home in the country rushed back into her thoughts; eagerly she drank in the sights around her, while a feverish desire seized her and carried her through the wondrous halls.

She was tired, and her fatigue increased. She felt a yearning to rest on the soft Oriental cushions and carpets, or to duck into the clear water as did the branches of the weeping willow. But the mayfly has no rest. In a few minutes the day would end. Her thoughts and her limbs trembled, and she sank in the grass beside the babbling stream.

"You spring from the earth with eternal life," she said. "Cool my tongue; give me a refreshing drink!"

"I am no living spring," answered the water. "I run by machinery!"

"Give me some of your freshness, you green grass!" begged the Dryad. "Give me one of the fragrant flowers!"

"We shall die if we are torn from our plants," answered

grass blade and flower.

"Kiss me, you cooling breeze! Give me but a single kiss!"

"Soon the sun will kiss the clouds red," said the wind, "and then you will be among the dead, gone as all this glory will be gone before the year is out. And then I can once more play with the light, loose sand in this place and blow the dust over the earth and into the air. Dust! Nothing but dust!"

The Dryad felt a terror creep over her, like a woman who, bleeding to death in the bath from a severed artery, still wishes to live, while her strength gradually leaves her from loss of blood. She rose, staggered a few steps forward, and then sank again before a little church. The door was open; a light burned on the altar, and the organ sounded. What music! The Dryad never had heard such tones before, though she seemed to hear familiar voices; they came from the depths of the great heart of creation. She thought she heard the whistling of the old oak tree; she thought she heard the old pastor speaking of the great deeds of famous men and of what a creation of God could and might give to the coming ages and thus win himself eternal life. The tones of the organ swelled and rang out; they spoke in song:

"Your desire and longing tore your roots from the place God had given them. That became your ruin, poor Dryad!"

Then the tones from the organ grew soft and gentle; they sounded like weeping and then died away like a weeping whisper. The clouds in the sky began to redden with the dawn. The wind whispered, and sang, "Go away, you dead, for the sun is rising!" The first ray fell upon the Dryad; her figure was radiant with changing colors, like a soap bubble before it bursts, vanishes, and becomes a drop, a tear, which falls and disappears. Poor Dryad, a dewdrop, only a tear, wept, and swept away!

The sun shone down on the Champ de Mars' Fata Morgana, shone over mighty Paris, over the little square with its trees and its rippling fountain, and between the high houses, where the chestnut tree stood, its branches now drooping, its leaves withered, the tree that only yesterday had stood as erect and fresh as spring itself. It was dead now, said the people, for the Dryad had left it, had passed away like the clouds—where, no one knew. On the ground there lay a withered, crumpled chestnut blossom. All the holy water of the church could not recall it to life. Human feet soon stepped on it and crushed it into the dust.

All this has happened and been experienced. We ourselves have seen it, at the Paris Exposition in 1867, in our time, the great and wonderful time of fairy tales.

GODFATHER'S PICTURE BOOK (1868)

Godfather could tell stories, so many of them and such long ones, and he could cut out paper figures and draw pictures. When it was nearly Christmas he would bring out a scrapbook with clean white pages, and on these he pasted pictures cut out of books and newspapers; and if there weren't enough for the story he was going to tell, he drew them himself. When I was a little boy I got several of these picture books, but the prettiest of them all was the one from "that memorable year when gas replaced the old oil lamps in Copenhagen"—and that was the inscription written on the first page.

"We must take great care of this book," said Father and Mother, "and only bring it out on important occasions."

But Godfather had written on the cover:

If you should tear the book, that's not a great wrong;

Other little friends have done worse for ever so long.

Best of all were the times when Godfather himself showed the book, read the verses and other writings in it, and told many things besides; then the story would become a very real one.

On the first page was a picture from "The Flying Post," showing Copenhagen with its Round Tower and Our Lady's Church. On its left was pasted an old lantern, on which was written, "Train oil," and on the right was a chandelier, with "Gas" written on it.

"See, that's the title page," said Godfather. "That's the beginning of the story you're going to hear. It could also be given as an entire play, if one could perform it. Train Oil and Gas; or, The Life and Times of Copenhagen. That's a very good title! At the bottom of the page is still another little picture; it's quite hard to understand, so I'll explain it to you. That is a hell horse. He shouldn't have come until the end of the book, but he has run on ahead to say that neither the beginning, nor the middle, nor the end is any good; he could have done it much better—if he could have done it at all. The hell horse, you see, stands hitched all day in the newspaper, and walks on the columns, they say. But in the evening he slips out, stations himself outside the poet's door, and neighs, so that the man inside will instantly die; but he won't die if there's any real life in him."

The hell horse is usually a poor creature who can't understand himself and can't earn a living, and he gets his air and food by going around and neighing. I am certain that he doesn't like Godfather's picture book, but in spite of that, it may be worth at least the paper it's written on.

"Now that's the first page of the book; that's the title page. "It was the very last evening on which the oil lamps were to be lighted; the town had gas, and it was so bright that the old street lamps seemed quite lost in it.

"I was in the street myself that evening," said Godfather. "The people were walking about, looking at the old and the new lighting. There were a great many people and twice as many legs as heads. The watchmen stood around sadly, for they didn't know how soon they would be dismissed, like the oil lamps. They could remember so far back, but dared not think forward. They had so many memories of quiet evenings and dark nights. I leaned up against a lamppost," continued

Godfather, "and there was a great spluttering in the oil and the wick. I could hear what the lamp said, and you shall hear it, too.

"'We've done the best we could,' said the lamp. 'We were good enough for our time, and have lighted up joy and sorrow; we have lived through many wonderful things; you might say we have been the night eyes of Copenhagen. Now let new lights take our place and take over our duties; but how many years they'll shine, and what they will light up, remains to be seen! Indeed, they shine a little stronger than we old fellows, but that's nothing; when you're molded like a gas chandelier and have the connections they have, the one pours into the other. They have pipes going in all directions and can get strength from both inside the town and outside it. But each one of us oil lamps shines because of what he has in himself, and not because of any family connections. We and our ancestors have lighted Copenhagen from olden times, from immeasurably long ago. But since this is now the last evening that we'll stand and shine in the second row, so to speak, in the street here along with you, you shining comrades, we won't sulk or be envious. No, far from it; we'll be happy and good-natured. We are the old sentinels, being relieved by new guards in better uniforms than ours. We'll tell you what our family, way back to great-great-great-grandmother lantern, has seen and experienced—the whole history of Copenhagen. May you and your successors, right down to the last gas chandelier, experience and be able to relate such wonderful things as we can, when you get your discharge someday. And you'll get it!

'You may be sure of that! People are certain to find a better light than gas. I've heard a student say that there's a possibility they may someday burn seawater!' When the lamp said these words, the wick spluttered, as if it had water in it already."

Godfather had listened closely, thought it over, and decided it was an excellent idea of the old lantern, on this evening of the change from oil to gas, to tell and display the whole history of Copenhagen.

"You mustn't let a good idea slip," said Godfather. "I took it at once, went home, and made this picture book for you. It goes even farther back in time than the lamps could go. Here's the book, and here's the story!"

COPENHAGEN'S LIFE AND TIMES

"It begins in darkness, on a coal-black page—that's the Dark Ages. "Now let's turn the page," said Godfather. "Do you see the picture? Only the wild sea and the swelling northeast wind, driving heavy ice floes before it. There's no one out sailing on them, only great stone blocks, which rolled down onto the ice from the mountains of Norway. The north wind blows the ice away; he wants to show the German mountains what rocks are found up in the north. The ice floes are already down in the sound, off the coast of Zealand, where Copenhagen now stands; but there was no Copenhagen there then. There were great sandbanks under the water, and the ice floes with the big boulders struck against one of these. Then the whole ice field stuck so fast that the northeast wind couldn't move it again, and so he became as furious as could be and pronounced a curse on the sandbank, the 'Thieves' ground,' as he called it. He swore that if ever it should rise above the surface of the sea, thieves and robbers would live there, and the gallows and wheel be raised on it.

"But while he cursed and swore this way, the sun came out, and those bright and gentle spirits, the children of light, swayed and swung in its beams; they danced over the ice floes until they melted, and the great boulders sank to the sandy bottom of the sea.

"'Sun scum!' said the northeast wind. 'Is that friendship and kinship? I'll remember and take revenge for that. Now I pronounce a curse!'

"'We pronounce a blessing!' sang the children of light. 'The sandbank will rise, and we shall guard it. Truth, goodness, and beauty shall dwell there!'

"'Stuff and nonsense!' said the northeast wind.

"You see, the lantern knew nothing of all this and therefore couldn't tell about it," said Godfather. "But I know it, and it's very important to the life and times of Copenhagen.

"Now we'll turn the page," said Godfather. "Years have passed, and the sandbank has lifted itself; a sea gull has settled on the biggest rock, which has jutted out of water. You can see it in the picture. Years and years have passed.

"The sea cast up dead fish onto the shore. Tough lyme grass sprang up, withered, rotted, and fertilized the soil; many different kinds of grasses and plants followed, until the bank became a green island. There the Vikings landed, for there was level ground for fighting and good anchorage beside the island off the coast of Zealand.

"I think the first oil lamp was lit to cook fish over, and there were plenty of fishes here. The herring swam through the sound in great shoals; it was hard to force a boat through them. They glittered in the water as if there were lightning down there, and shone in the depths like the northern lights. The sound had a wealth of fishes; therefore houses were built on the coast of Zealand, with walls of oak and roofs of bark—there were trees enough for that purpose. Ships anchored in the harbor, oil lamps hanging from swaying ropes, and the northeast wind blew and sang, 'O-out!' If a lantern glimmered on the island it was a thieves' lantern, for smugglers and thieves plied their trade on Thieves' Island.

"'I believe that all the evil I wished for is coming,' said the northeast wind. 'Soon the tree will come, from which I can shake the fruit.'

"And here is the tree," said Godfather. "Do you see the gallows on Thieves' Island? Robbers and murderers hang there in iron chains, exactly as they hung in those days. The wind blew until it rattled the long skeletons, but the moon shone down on them as serenely as it now shines on a country dance. The sun also shone down pleasantly, crumbling away the dangling skeletons, and from the sunbeams the children of light sang, 'We know it! We know it! Here it shall be beautiful in the days to come; here it shall be good and splendid!'

"'Chicken prattle!' said the northeast wind.

"Now we'll turn the page," said Godfather.

"The bells were ringing in the town of Roskilde, where Bishop Absalon lived. He could both read his Bible and wield his sword; he had power and will. He wished to protect from assault the busy fishermen at the harbor, whose town had grown until it was now a market town. He sprinkled the unhallowed ground with holy water; thus, Thieves' Island received the mark of honor. Masons and carpenters set to work on it; at the bishop's command, a building grew up, and the sunbeams kissed the red walls as they rose. There stood the house of Axel:

The castle, with its towers, so stately and high,
Had balconies and stairs up to the sky
Booo! Whooo!
The northeast wind huffed and puffed,
But the castle stood unyielding, unruffed.

"And outside it lay 'The Haven,' the merchants' harbor:

Mermaid's bower amid seas of sheen,
Built beside groves of green.

"The foreigners came there and bought the wealth of fish, and built shops and houses with bladders for windowpanes, as glass was too expensive. Warehouses followed, with gables and windlasses. See the old fellows sitting there in the shops—they dare not marry; they trade in ginger and pepper, the pebersvende.

"The northeast wind whistled through the streets and lanes, sending the dust flying and tearing off a thatched roof. Cows and pigs wandered about in the street ditch.

"'I shall tame and subdue them!' said the northeast wind. 'I'll whistle around the houses and around Axel's house! I can't fail! They call it Gallows' Castle on Thieves' Island.'"

Then Godfather showed a picture of it, which he himself had drawn. On the wall were rows of stakes, and on every stake was the head of a captured pirate showing its teeth.

"That really happened," said Godfather. "And it's worth hearing and worth knowing about.

"Bishop Absalon was in his bath, and through the thin walls he heard the arrival of a ship of freebooters. He instantly sprang out of the bath and into his ship, blew his horn, and his crew assembled. The arrows shot into the backs of the robbers as they rowed desperately to escape. The arrows pierced into their hands, and there was no time to pull them out. Bishop Absalon caught everyone and cut their heads off, and every head was set up on the outer wall of the castle. The northeast wind blew with puffed-out cheeks—with bad weather in his jaw, as the sailors say.

"'I'll stretch myself,' said the wind. 'Here I'll lie down and look the whole matter over.'

"It rested for hours, then blew for days. Years went past. "The watchman appeared on the castle tower; he looked to the east, the west, the north, and the south. You can see it there in the picture," said Godfather, pointing it out. "You can see him there, but I'll tell you what he saw.

"There is open water from the wall of Stejleborg right out to Kjöge Bay, and a broad channel over to the coast of Zealand. In front of Serritslev and Solberg Meadows, with their large villages, the new town, with its gabled timber houses, is growing up more and more. There are entire streets for shoemakers and tailors, for grocers and beer sellers; there is a marketplace and there is a guildhall, and near the shore, where there was once an island, stands the splendid Church of St. Nicolaus. It has an immensely high tower and spire; how it is reflected in the clear water! Near this is Our Lady's Church, where Masses are sung, where incense gives out its fragrance and wax candles burn. The 'merchants' haven' is now the bishop's town; the bishop of Roskilde rules and reigns there.

"Bishop Erlandsen sits in Axel's house. There is good cooking in the kitchen; ale and claret are served to the sound of fiddles and kettledrums. Burning candles and lamps make the castle shine as if it were a lantern for the whole country and kingdom. The northeast wind whistles around the tower and walls, but they stand firmly. The northeast wind swoops around the western fortification of the town—only an old wooden fence—but it holds up well. Christopher I, King of Denmark, stands outside it; the rebels have beaten him at Skelskör, so he seeks shelter in the bishop's town.

"The wind whistles, and says, like the bishop, 'Keep out! Keep out! The gate is shut to you!'

"It is a time of trouble, dismal days, when every man is his own master. The Holstein banner waves from the castle tower. There is want and woe, for it is the night of anguish. War and the black death stalk the land in the pitch-dark night—but then comes Valdemar Atterdag. Now the bishop's town is the king's town. It has gabled houses and narrow streets, watchmen and a town hall, and a permanent gallows by the west port. No man from out of town can be hanged on it; you must be a citizen to be allowed to dangle there, to get so high as to see Kjöge and the hens of Kjöge.

"'That's a lovely gallows,' says the northeast wind. 'The beautiful is growing!' And it whistles and whoops.

"And from Germany blew trouble and want.

"The Hanseatic merchants came," continued Godfather, "from warehouse and counter, the rich traders of Rostock, Lübeck, and Bremen. They wanted to seize more than the golden goose from Valdemar's Tower; they had more power in the town of the Danish king than the Danish king himself. They came in armed ships, and no one was prepared. And King Eric had no desire to fight with his German kinsfolk; they were too many and too strong. So King Eric and all his courtiers escaped through the west port to the town of Sorö, to the quiet lake and green forests, to the song of love and the clang of goblets.

"But there was one left behind in Copenhagen, a kingly heart and a kingly mind. Do you see this picture here, this young woman, so fine and tender, with sea-blue eyes and yellow hair? It is the Queen of Denmark, Philippa, the English princess. She stayed in the distracted city, where the townspeople swarmed in panic in the narrow lanes and streets with steep stairs, sheds, and shops of lath and plaster. With the courage of a man, she summoned townspeople and peasants, to inspire and encourage them. They fitted out the ships and garrisoned the blockhouses; they fired with their carbines; there were fire and smoke and lightness of spirit—our Lord will never forsake Denmark! The sun shone into all hearts, and in all eyes was the bright gladness of victory. Blessed be Philippa! Blessed she was in hut and in house; and blessed she was in the king's castle, where she nursed the wounded and the sick. I have clipped a wreath and laid it around this picture," said Godfather. "Blessed be Queen Philippa!"

"Now we spring forward for years," said Godfather, "and Copenhagen springs with us. King Christian I has been to Rome to receive the Pope's blessing and has been greeted with honor and homage on the long journey. Here at home he is building a hall of red brick; there shall be learning there, displaying itself in Latin. The poor man's children, from plow and workshop, can also come there, to live upon alms, to attain the long black gown, and sing before the doors of citizens.

"Near the hall of learning, where everything is in Latin, is a little house where Danish rules, in language and in customs.

There is beer soup for early breakfast, and dinner is at ten o'clock in the morning. The sun shines through small panes onto cupboards and bookcases; on the shelves are written treasures—Master Mikkel's Rosary and Godly Comedies, Henrik Harpestreng's Leech-book, and Denmark's Rhyming Chronicle by Brother Niels of Sorö. 'Every Danish man should know these,' says the master of the house, and he is the one to make them known. He is the Dutchman, Gotfred van Gehmen, Denmark's first printer, who practices the divine black art of printing.

"And the books enter the castle of the king and the houses of the citizens. Proverbs and songs are given immortality. Things that men dare not say either in sorrow or in joy are sung by the Bird of Folklore, allegorically and yet clearly. For it flies free and wide through the common man's room and the knightly castle; it sits and twitters like a falcon on the hand of the noble lady; it steals in like a tiny mouse and squeaks in the dungeon of the enslaved peasant.

"'Merely words—all of it!' says the sharp northeast wind. "'It's the spring!' say the sunbeams. 'See how the green buds are peeping out!' "Now we'll turn more pages in our picture book," said Godfather. "How radiant Copenhagen is! There are tournaments and sports and splendid processions! Look at the gallant knights in armor and the noble ladies in silk and gold! King Hans gives his daughter, Elizabeth, to the Elector of Brandenburg. How young she is, and how happy she is! She is treading on velvet; there is a whole future in her thoughts—a future of domestic happiness. Close beside her is her royal brother, Prince Christian, with the melancholy eyes and the hot, passionate blood. He is beloved by the commoners, for he knows their burdens; in his thoughts, he has the poor man's future. God alone decides our fate!

"Now we'll turn another leaf in the picture book," said Godfather. "The wind blows sharply and sings of the sharp sword and this difficult time of trouble.

"It is an icy-cold day in mid-April. Why is the crowd gathering outside the castle and before the old customhouse, where the king's ship lies with its sails and banners? People are crowded in the windows and on the roofs. There are sorrow and trouble, expectation and anxiety. They look toward the castle, now so still and empty, but where formerly there were torch dances in the gilded halls; they look at the balcony from which King Christian so often gazed out over the 'court bridge' and down the narrow court-bridge street to his dovelet, the little Dutch girl he brought from the town of Bergen. The shutters are bolted. As the crowd gazed toward the castle, the gate is opened and the drawbridge is let down. There comes King Christian with his faithful wife, Elizabeth; she will not forsake her royal lord, now when he is so hard pressed.

"There is fire in his blood and fire in his thoughts; he has wished to break with the olden times, to strike off the peasants' yoke, to do good to the commoners, to clip the wings of the 'greedy hawks,' but they have been too much for him. He leaves his country and his kingdom, to win allies and friends for himself abroad. His wife and loyal men go with him. Every eye is moist in this hour of parting.

"Voices are blended in the song of time, against him and for him a three-part choir. "Listen to the words of the nobles; they are written and printed: 'Woe to you, Christian the Wicked! The blood that poured out in the marketplace of Stockholm cries aloud and curses you!'

"And the monks' cry echoes the same refrain: 'Be you cast off by God and by us! You have called hither the Lutheran doctrine; you have given it church and pulpit and bid the tongue of the Devil speak out! Woe to you, Christian the Wicked!'

"But the peasants and commoners weep: 'Christian, beloved of the people! No longer may the peasant be sold like cattle or exchanged for a hunting hound! That law shall bear you witness!' But the words of the poor man are only chaff before the wind.

"Now the ship sails past the castle, and the commoners line the ramparts, so that they may once more see the royal galley sail.

"'The time is long; the time is hard. Trust neither in friends nor in kinsmen!'

"Uncle Frederick in the Castle of Kiel would like to be King of Denmark. King Frederick is before Copenhagen. See the picture here—'The Faithful Copenhagen.' Coal-black clouds are around it—in picture after picture; just look at each of them! It is all a resounding picture; it resounds still in song and story—those heavy, hard, and bitter times during the long procession of years.

"How did it go with that wandering bird, King Christian? The birds have sung about it, and they fly far over distant lands and seas.

"Early in the spring the stork came from the south, across the land of Germany; it had seen what I will tell you now.

"'I saw the fugitive King Christian crossing a heather-grown moor; he met a wretched cart drawn by only one horse. A woman sat in it, his sister, the Countess of Brandenburg. Faithful to the Lutheran religion, she had been exiled by her husband. And so on that dark heath, the exiled children of a king met. The time is hard; the time is long. Trust neither friend nor kinsman!'

"The swallow came from Sönderborg Castle with a sad song, 'King Christian is betrayed! He sits in the dungeon tower, deep as a well; his heavy steps wear tracks in the stone floor, and his fingers leave their marks in the hard marble.'

Oh, what sorrow ever found such vent
As that in the furrows of the stone?

"The fish eagle has come from the tossing sea, which is open and free. A ship flies over it, bearing the brave Sören Norby from Fyn. Fortune is with him—but fortune is as changeable as wind and weather.

"In Jutland and Fyn the crows and ravens scream, 'We seek spoil! It is grand! Caw, caw! Here lie the bodies of horses and of men, too!' It is a time of trouble; it is during the Count of Oldenburg's war. The peasant raises his club and the townsman his knife, and loudly they shout, 'We shall slay the wolves and leave no cub of them alive!' Clouds of smoke roll up from the burning towns.

"King Christian is a prisoner in Sönderborg Castle; he cannot escape or see the bitter distress of Copenhagen. On the North Common stands Christian III, where his father stood before him. Despair is in the city, and plague, and famine.

"A ragged, emaciated woman sits reclined against the church wall. She is a corpse; two living children lie on her lap and can suck only blood from the dead breast.

"Courage has collapsed; resistance collapses. Oh, you faithful Copenhagen!

"Fanfares are blown; hear the drums and trumpets! In rich garments of silk and velvet, with nodding plumes, the noble lords come on horses adorned with gold, riding to Old Market Square. Is there a customary festivity or tournament? Commoners and peasants in holiday attire flock in that direction. What is there to see? Is there a bonfire to burn popish images? Or is the hangman standing there, as he stood at the death fire of Slaghoek? The king, ruler of all the land, is a Lutheran, and this shall now be proclaimed with solemnity.

"Noble ladies and highborn maidens, with high collars and caps of pearls, sit behind the open windows and see all the splendor. Beneath a canopy near the king's throne, the councillors of state sit in antique dress on an outspread carpet. The king is silent, but his will, the will of the council of state, is proclaimed in the Danish tongue. Commoners and peasants are sternly rebuked for the opposition they have shown to the nobility. The commoner is humbled, and the peasant becomes a slave. Now condemning words are uttered against the bishops of the land. Their power is gone, and all the property of the church and cloisters is transferred to the king and the nobles.

"Pride and hatred are there, and pomp and misery, too.

The poor bird comes limping, drooping,
Comes stooping.
The rich bird comes huffing,
Comes puffing.

"The time of change brings heavy clouds, but sunshine, too; it then shines in the halls of learning and in the student's home. And names shine from it on down to our own days. There is Hans Tousen, the son of a poor smith of Fyn:

This was the little lad who came from Birkende town;
His name flew over Denmark; widely spread his renown.
A Danish Martin Luther, he drew the Gospel sword,
And gained a mighty victory for truth and for the Lord.

"There is also the immortal name of Petrus Palladius; that is the Latin, but in Danish, it is Peter Plade, Bishop of Roskilde, also the son of a poor smith of Jutland. And among noblemen shines the name of Hans Friis, chancellor of the kingdom. He would seat the students at his own table and see to their wants and those of the schoolboys as well. But one name above all others is greeted with cheers and song.

So long as there's a student to be found
Near Axel's Haven, at work or play,
Will King Christian's name loudly resound
And with hurrahs be greeted every day!

"Yes, there were sunbeams between the heavy clouds in the time of change.

"Now we turn the page.

"What is it that whistles and sings in the Great Belt under the coast of Samsö? A mermaid, with sea-green hair, rises from the sea; she reveals the future to the peasant. A prince shall be born who shall become a great and powerful king."

"He was born in the field, beneath the blossoming whitethorn. His name now lives in song and story, in the knightly halls and castles everywhere. The stock exchange came forth with tower and spire; Rosenborg Castle rose up and gazed far out over the ramparts; the students got their own house. And close by, where it still points to heaven, stood 'the Round Tower,' facing toward the island of Hveen, where Uranienborg once stood. Its golden domes glittered in the moonlight, and the mermaids sang of the man who lived there, whom kings and sages visited, the master sage of noble blood—Tycho Brahe. He raised the name of Denmark so high that it was known with the stars of Heaven in all the cultured lands of Earth. And Denmark turned him away.

"In his sorrow he sang for comfort:

Is not Heaven everywhere?

What more do I require?

"His song lives in the hearts of the people, like the mermaid's song about Christian IV.

"Now comes a page that you must look at carefully," said Godfather.

"There is picture after picture here, just as there is verse after verse in the old ballads. It is a song, so happy in its beginning, so sorrowful at its close.

"A king's child is dancing in the castle of the king. How lovely she is to look at! She is sitting on the lap of Christian IV—his beloved daughter, Eleonore. She grows in all the virtues and graces of a woman. The foremost among the nobles, Corfits Ulfeldt, is her betrothed. She is still only a child and is beaten by her stern governess; she complains of this to her sweetheart, and rightly, too. How clever and cultured and learned she is! She can speak Latin and Greek, sing in Italian to her lute, and talk about the Pope and Martin Luther.

"Now King Christian lies in the vault in Roskilde Cathedral, and Eleonore's brother is king. In the palace at Copenhagen there are pomp and show; there are beauty and wit—and foremost is the queen herself, Sophie Amalie of Lyneborg. Who can guide her horse as cleverly as she? Who dances with such grace? Who can talk with such wisdom and wit as the Queen of Denmark?

"'Eleonore Christine Ulfeldt!' These are the words of the French Ambassador. 'She surpasses all in beauty and wit!'

"Up from the polished floor of the palace ballroom has grown the burdock of envy; it has clung there, worked itself in, and twisted around—contempt and scorn. 'That illegitimate creature! Her carriage shall stop at the bridge of the castle! Where the queen drives, the commoner shall walk!' There is a storm of gossip, of lies and slander.

"Then Ulfeldt takes his wife by the hand in the still of the night. He has the keys to the town gates; he opens one of them, and horses wait outside. They ride to the shore and sail to Sweden.

"Now let's turn the page, just as fortune turned itself for those two.

"It is autumn. The days are short and the nights are long; it is gray and damp. The cold wind rises in its strength, and it whistles through the leaves of the trees on the ramparts. The leaves drop into Peter Oxe's courtyard, empty and forsaken of its owners. The wind sweeps over Christianshavn, around the mansion of Kai Lykke, which now is a penitentiary. He himself has been driven from home and honor; his escutcheon is smashed and his effigy hung on the highest gallows. Thus is he punished for his thoughtless, frivolous words about the powerful Queen of Denmark. The wind pipes loudly as it rushes over the open space where the mansion of the Lord High Steward once stood. Only one stone of it is now left. 'And that I drove down here as a boulder on the floating ice,' shrieks the wind. 'That stone stranded where since has grown Thieves' Island, under my curse, and so it became a part of the mansion of Lord Ulfeldt, where his lady sang to the sounding lute, and read Greek and Latin, and bore herself proudly. Now only the stone is here with its inscription:

The traitor Corfits Ulfeldt
In eternal scorn, shame, and disgrace.

"'But where is the stately lady now? Whoo-ee-oo!' blows the wind with a piercing shriek.

"For many years she has been shut up in the Blue Tower, behind the palace, where the sea water beats against the slimy walls. There is more smoke than warmth in the cell; its tiny window is high up under the ceiling. In what discomfort and misery sits the adored child of Christian IV, the daintiest of maids and matrons! Memory hangs curtains and tapestries on the smoke-blackened walls of her prison. She recalls the lovely days of her childhood, her father's gentle, beaming face; she recalls her splendid wedding, her days of pride, but also her days of misery in Holland, England, and Bornholm.

Nothing seems too hard for wedded love to bear,
And loyalty is not cause for shame or care.

"But he was with her in those days; now she is alone, alone forever. She does not know his grave; no one knows it.

Faithfulness to her husband was her only crime.

"For long and many years she sat there, while life went on outside. Life never pauses, but we will for a moment here, and think of her and the words of the song.

I keep my promise to my husband still,
In want and dire need, and always will.

"Now do you see this picture here?" said Godfather. "It's winter, and the frost has thrown a bridge of ice between Laaland and Fyn, a bridge for Carl Gustav, who pushes on unchecked. There are plundering and burning, fear and want, throughout the whole land.

"Now the Swedes are encamped before Copenhagen. It is bitterly cold and the snow is blinding, but, true to their king and themselves, men and women stand ready to fight. Every tradesman, shopman, student, and schoolmaster is on the ramparts, ready to guard and defend, with no fear of the red-hot cannon balls. King Frederick has sworn he will die in his nest. There he rides to and fro, and the queen is with him, and courage, patriotism, and discipline are there. Let the Swede don his white shroud and crawl forward in the white snow and try to storm the walls! Beams and stones are hurled down on him; even women come with steaming caldrons and pour boiling pitch and tar onto the storming enemy.

"That night, king and peasant are one united power. Then there is relief, and there is victory. Church bells ring, and songs of thanksgiving resound. Commoners, on this spot you won your knightly spurs!

"What comes next? Look at this picture. Bishop Svane's wife drives in a closed carriage, which only the high and mighty nobility dare do. The proud young men stop the carriage; the bishop's wife must walk to the bishop's house.

"Is that the whole story? Something much greater is stopped next—the power of pride.

"Burgomaster Hans Nansen and Bishop Svane clasp hands to work in the name of the Lord. Their wise and honest talk is heard in the church and the house of the commoner. One handclasp of fellowship, and the harbor is blocked, the gates are locked, and the alarm bell rings.

"Power is granted to the king alone, who remains in his nest in the hour of peril; he governs, and rules over great and small. It is the time of absolute monarchy.

"Now let's turn the page, and time with it.

"'Halloo, halloo, halloo!' The plow stands idle, and the heather grows wild, but the hunting is good. 'Halloo, halloo!' Listen to the sounding horn and the baying hounds! See the huntsmen, and look at the young and gay king himself, Christian V! There is merrymaking in palace and in town. In the halls are waxlights, in the courtyards torches, and in the streets of the town are new lamps. Everything is so new! Favors and gifts go to the barons and counts of the new nobility, brought in from Germany. Nothing is accepted now except titles and rank and the German language.

"But then there sounds a voice that is truly Danish, the voice of the weaver's son, who is now a bishop; it is the voice of Kingo, singing his beautiful psalms.

"There is another commoner's son, this time the son of a vintner, whose thoughts shine forth in law and justice. His book of laws has become gold-ground for the king's name, and will stand for ages to come. That commoner's son, the greatest man in the land, receives a coat of arms—and enemies as well, so that the sword of the executioner is raised over the head of Griffenfeld.

"But mercy is granted, with life imprisonment, and he is banished to a rocky islet off the coast of Trondhjem.

Munkholm—Denmark's St. Helena

"But the dance continues merrily in the palace hall; there are splendor and pomp there, and courtiers and ladies dance to lively music.

"Now these are the times of Frederick IV!

"See the proud ships with their flags of victory! See the tossing sea! It can tell of great deeds for the glory of Denmark. We remember the victorious Sehested and Gyldenlöve! We remember Hvitfeldt, who blew up his ship to save the Danish fleet, and flew to Heaven with Dannebrog. We think of the struggles of those ages, and of the hero who sprang to the defense of Denmark from the mountains of Norway—Peder Tordenskjold.

Across the surging sea his name thunders from country to country.

Lightning flashed through the powder dust;
A thunderbolt roared through the whispering age.
A tailor's boy jumped down from the tailor's table;
From Norway's coast he sailed a little sloop.
And over Northern seas there flew again
The Viking spirit, youthful, and clad in steel.

"Then a fresh breeze blew from the coast of Greenland, bringing a gentle fragrance, as if from the land of Bethlehem; it brought tidings of the gospel light kindled by Hans Egede and his wife.

"So this half page has a golden ground; but the other half, which means sorrow, is ashen gray with black specks, as from fire and disease and pestilence.

"The plague is raging in Copenhagen. The streets are empty. The doors are barred, and where crosses are chalked on them the plague is inside, but where the cross is black all within are dead.

"The bodies are carried away by night, with no tolling bell; the half dead in the streets are taken with them. Funeral wagons rumble, piled with corpses. But from the taverns sound the horrid songs and wild shrieks of the drunkards. They try to forget their bitter in drink; they want to forget, and end—end! Yes, everything comes to an end. The page ends here, with the second time of distress and trial for Copenhagen.

"King Frederick IV is still alive. The course of the years has turned his hair gray. From the window of his palace he looks out on the stormy weather of late winter.

"In a little house near the Westgate a boy is playing with his ball; it bounces up into the loft. The child takes a candle and goes up to seek it, but he sets fire to the little house—to the whole street. The fire leaps into the air so that the clouds themselves reflect it! See how the flames grow higher! There is food for the fire—hay and straw, bacon and tar, piles of firewood for winter—and it all burns. There is weeping, shrieking; there is great panic. The old king rides through the tumult, commanding and encouraging. There is blowing up with gunpowder, and the tearing down of houses. Now the fire has swept into the north quarter, and the churches are burning, St. Peter's and Our Lady's. Listen to the bells playing their last tune, 'Turn from Us Thy Wrath, O Lord God of Mercy!'

"Only the Round Tower and the castle are left standing, with smoking ruins about them. King Frederick is kind to the people; he is a friend to the homeless; he comforts and feeds them and is with them constantly. Blessed be Frederick IV!

"Now look at this page! "See that gilded carriage with footmen around it and armed riders before and behind it, coming from the castle, where an iron chain is stretched to keep the people from coming too near! Every common man must cross the square with bare head; and therefore few are seen there; they avoid the place. There comes one now, with downcast eyes, and with hat in hand, and he is the one man of that time whom we can name with pride:

His voice like a cleansing storm wind rang.
To sunshine in the days which yet were to come!
Then smuggled-in tunes like grasshoppers sprang
In haste to return to where they were from.

"Witty and humorous—that is Ludvig Holberg. The Danish stage, the castle of his greatness, has been closed as if it were the dwelling place of shame. All merriment is banished; dance, song, and music are forbidden and gone. For the dark side of religion is now in power.

"'The Danish prince!' his mother used to call him. Now come his days of sunshine, with the song of birds, with gladness and true Danish gaiety. Frederick V is king, and the chain is taken from the square beside the castle; the Danish theater is re-opened; there are laughter and pleasure and good cheer. And the peasants again hold their summer festivals, for it is a time of joy after the time of fasting and oppression. The beautiful lives again, blossoming and bearing fruit in sound, color, and creative art. Listen to Grétry's music! Watch Londemann's acting! And Denmark's queen loves all that is Danish. God in his Heaven bless you, beautiful and gentle Louise of England! The sunbeams sing in spirited chorus about the queens of Denmark—Philippa, Elizabeth, Louise!

"The earthly shells have long been buried, but the souls live, and the names live. England again sends a royal bride, Matilde, so young and so soon forsaken! In days to come poets will sing of your youthful heart and your hours of trail! And song has an indescribable power through all times and all peoples. See the burning of the castle of King Christian! They try to save the best they can find. Look at the men from the dockyard dragging away a basket of silverware and precious things—a great treasure! But suddenly through an open door, where the flames are brightest, they see a bronze bust of King Christian IV. Then they cast aside the treasure they are rescuing; his image means so much more to them that it must be saved, regardless of how heavy it may be to carry. They know him from the song of Ewald and the beautiful melody of Hartmann.

"Indeed, there is power in words and song, and someday it shall resound as strongly for the poor Queen Matilde.

"Now let's go further in our picture book.

"On Ulfeldt's Place stood the stone of shame, and where in the world is there one like it? By the Westgate a column was raised, and how many in the world are there like it?

"The sunbeams kissed the boulder foundation of the Column of Freedom. All church bells rang and the flags waved, and the people cheered for Crown Prince Frederick. The names of Bernstorff, Reventlow, Colbjörnsen were held in the hearts and were on the lips of old and young. With bright eyes and grateful hearts they read the blessed inscription on the column:

"'The king has decreed that serfdom shall cease, the agrarian laws be set in order and enforced, so that the free peasant may become brave and enlightened, diligent and good, a worthy and happy citizen!'

"What a sunny day! Summer is in town!

"The spirits of light sang, 'The good is growing! The beautiful is growing! Soon the stone on Ulfeldt's Place shall fall, but the Column of Freedom shall stand in the sunlight, blessed by God, king, and people.'

We have an ancient highway;

It goes to the ends of the earth.

"There in the open sea—open for friend and foe—was the foe! The mighty English fleet sailed up; a great power came against a little one. The battle was hard, but the people were valiant.

Each stood firm, untiring, held his place,
Stood and fought until death's embrace.

"They won the admiration of the enemy and inspired the poets of Denmark. The day of that battle is still commemorated with unfurled banners—Denmark's glorious Second of April, the Maundy Thursday battle at Copenhagen Harbor.

"Years passed. A fleet was seen in Öresund. Was it bound for Russia or for Denmark? No one knew, not even those on board the ships.

"There is a legend in the hearts of the people which tells that on that morning in Öresund, when the sealed orders were opened and the instructions to destroy the Danish fleet were read, a young captain stepped forward, a son of Britain, noble in word and deed. 'I swore,' he said, 'that I would fight for England's flag to my death, in open and honorable battle, but not overpower the weak!' And with that he jumped overboard!

The fleet sailed toward Copenhagen just the same;
But far from the place where the battle was to be
Lay he, the captain—and unknown is his name—
An ice-cold corpse, in the dark-blue sea.
Shoreward he drifted, until Swedish men,
Fishing beneath the stars with their nets,
Found him, bore him to shore, and then
Cast dice to win his epaulets!

"The enemy made for Copenhagen. The town was soon in

flames. We lost our fleet, but not our courage and faith in God; He casteth down but He raiseth again. Our wounds healed, as those of the warriors in Valhalla. The history of Copenhagen is rich in consolation.

Our faith, from the beginning of time to the end,
Is that Our Lord is Denmark's friend;
If we hold firmly, He will hold, too,
And tomorrow the sun will shine on you.

"Soon the sun did shine on the rebuilt city, on the rich cornfields, and on the skill and art of our people. It was blessed summer day of peace, when poetry raised her Fata Morgana, so rich in color, through the words of Oehlenschläger.

"And a great discovery was made in science. It was a discovery far greater than the gold horn of ancient days, for a bridge of gold was found:

A bridge for thought to flash like lightning
At all times into other lands and nations.

"Hans Christian Örsted wrote his name on that bridge. And look! Beside the church by the castle, a building was raised to which the poorest man and woman gladly gave their pennies.

"You will remember that in the first part of our picture book," said Godfather, "the old stone blocks rolled down from the mountains of Norway and were carried here on the ice. They are raised up again from the sandy depths at the bidding of Thorvaldsen, in marble beauty, magnificent to look at!

"Remember all that I have shown you and all that I have told you! That sandbank in the sea raised itself up to become a breakwater in the harbor; it bore Axel's house, and the bishop's mansion, and the king's castle, and now it bears the temple of the beautiful. The words of the curse have vanished, but all that the children of sunlight sang in their gladness about the coming ages has been fulfilled. Many storms have passed; they will come again and pass again. The true and the good and the beautiful have the victory.

"And that finishes the picture book, but not the history of Copenhagen—far from it! Who knows what you may live to see! It has often looked black, and storms have raged, but the sunshine has never been blown away—it remains. And stronger yet than the brightest sunshine is God! Our Lord reigns over more than Copenhagen."

That is what Godfather said as he gave me the book. His eyes were shining; he was so certain of it all. And I took the book so gladly and proudly and carefully, just the way I carried my little sister for the first time.

And Godfather said, "You're quite welcome to show your picture book to people, and you may also tell them that I made it, pasted it, and drew the whole thing. But it's of great importance that they know at once where I got the idea for it. You know where, so tell them! The idea came from the old oil lamps, which, on the last evening they burned, showed the new gaslights, like a Fata Morgana, everything that had been seen from the time the first lamp was lit at the harbor until that evening when Copenhagen was lighted with both oil and gas.

"You may show the book to anybody you like; that is, to people with kindly eyes and friendly minds; but if a hell horse should come, then close Godfather's picture book."

THE RAGS (1868)

Outside the paper mill, masses of rags lay piled in high stacks; they had been gathered from far and wide. Every rag had a tale to tell, and told it, too; but we can't listen to all of them. Some of the rags were native; others came from foreign countries.

Now here lay a Danish rag beside a rag from Norway; one was decidedly Danish, the other decidedly Norse, and that was the amusing part about the two, as any good Dane or Norwegian could tell you. They could understand each other well enough, though the two languages were as different, according to the Norwegian, as French and Hebrew. "We go to the hills for our language, and there get it pure and firsthand, while the Dane cooks up some sort of a suckling-sweet lingo!"

So the rags talked—and a rag is a rag in every land the world over; they are considered of no value except in the rag heap.

"I am Norse!" said the Norwegian. "And when I've said I'm Norse I guess I've said enough. I'm firm of fiber, like the ancient granite rocks of old Norway. The land up there has a constitution, like the free United States. It makes my fibers tingle to think what I am and to sound out my thoughts in words of granite!"

"But we have literature," said the Danish rag. "Do you understand what that is?" "Understand?" repeated the Norwegian. "Lowland creature! Shall I give him a shove uphill and show him a northern light, rag that he is? When the sun of Norway has thawed the ice, then Danish fruit barges come up to us with butter and cheese—an eatable cargo, I grant you—but by way of ballast they bring Danish literature, too! We don't need the stuff. You don't need stale beer where fresh springs spout, and up there is a natural well that has never been tapped or been made known to Europeans by the cackling of newspapers, jobbers, and traveling authors in foreign countries. I speak freely from the bottom of my lungs, and the Dane must get used to a free voice. And so he will someday, when as a fellow Scandinavian he wants to cling to our proud mountain country, the summit of the world!"

"Now a Danish rag could never talk like that—never!" said the Dane. "It's not in our nature. I know myself, and all the other rags are like me. We're too good-natured, too unassuming; we think too little of ourselves. Not that we gain much by our modesty, but I like it; I think it's quite charming. Incidentally, I'm perfectly aware of my own good values, I assure you, but I don't talk about them; nobody can ever accuse me of that. I'm soft and easygoing; bear everything patiently, envy nobody, and speak good of everybody—though there isn't much good to be said of most other people, but that's their business. I can afford to smile at them; I know I'm so gifted."

"Don't speak to me in that lowland, pasteboard language—it makes me sick!" said the Norwegian, as he caught a puff of wind and fluttered away from his own heap to another.

They both became paper; and, as it turned out, the Norwegian rag became a sheet on which a Norwegian wrote a love letter to a Danish girl, while the Danish rag became the manuscript for a Danish poem praising Norway's beauty and strength.

So something good may come even of rags when they have once come out of the rag heap and the change has been made into truth and beauty; they keep up understanding relations between us, and in that there is a blessing.

That is the story. It's rather amusing and offends no one—but the rags.

WHICH WAS THE HAPPIEST? (1868)

Such lovely roses!" said the Sunshine. "And each bud will soon burst in bloom and be equally beautiful. These are my children. It is I who have kissed them to life."

"They are my children," said the Dew. "It is I who have nourished them with my tears."

"I should think I am their mother," the Rosebush said. "You and Sunshine are only their godmothers, who have made them presents in keeping with your means and your good will."

"My lovely Rose children!" they exclaimed, all three. They wished each flower to have the greatest happiness. But only one could be the happiest, and one must be the least happy. But which of them?

"I'll find out," said the Wind. "I roam far and wide. I find my way into the tiniest crevices. I know everything, inside and out."

Each rose in bloom heard his words, and each growing bud understood them.

Just then a sad devoted mother, in deep mourning, walked through the garden. She picked one of the roses; it was only half-blown but fresh and full. To her it seemed the loveliest of them all, and she took it to her quiet, silent room, where only a few days past her cheerful and lively young daughter had merrily tripped to and fro. Now she lay in the black coffin, as lifeless as a sleeping marble figure. The mother kissed her departed daughter. Then she kissed the half-blown rose and laid it on the young girl's breast, as if by its freshness and by the fond kiss of a mother, her beloved child's heart might again begin to beat.

The rose seemed to expand. Every petal trembled with joy. "What a lovely way has been set for me to go," it said. "Like a human child, I am given a mother's kiss and her blessing as I go to the blessed land unknown, dreaming upon the breast of Death's pale angel.

"Surely I am the happiest of all my sisters."

In the garden where the Rosebush grew walked an old woman whose business it was to weed the flower beds. She also looked at the beautiful bush, with especial interest in the largest full-blown rose. One more fall of dew, one more warm day, and its petals would shatter. When the old woman saw this she said that the rose had lived long enough for beauty, and that now she intended to put it to practical use. Then she picked it, wrapped it in old newspaper, and took it home, where she put it with other faded roses and those blue boys they call lavender, in a potpourri, embalmed in salt. Mind you, embalmed—an honor granted only to roses and kings.

"I will be the most highly honored," the rose declared, as the old weed puller took her. "I am the happiest one, for I am to be embalmed."

Then two young men came strolling through the garden. One was a painter; the other was a poet. Each plucked a rose most fair to see. The painter put upon canvas a likeness of the rose in bloom, a picture so perfect and so lovely that the rose itself supposed it must be looking into a mirror.

"In this way," said the painter, "it shall live on, for generations upon generations, while countless other roses fade and die."

"Ah!" said the rose, "after all, it is I who have been most highly favored. I had the best luck of all."

But the poet looked at his rose and wrote a poem about it to express the mystery of love. Yes, his book was a complete picture of love. It was a piece of immortal verse.

"This book has made me immortal," the rose said. "I am the most fortunate one."

In the midst of these splendid roses was one whom the others hid almost completely. By accident, and perhaps by good fortune, it had a slight defect. It sat slightly askew on its stem, and the leaves on one side of it did not match those on the other. Moreover, in the very heart of the flower grew a crippled leaf, small and green.

Such things happen, even to roses.

"Poor child," said the Wind, and kissed its cheek. The rose took this kiss for one of welcome and tribute. It had a feeling that it was made differently from the other roses, and that the green leaf growing in the heart of it was a mark of distinction. A butterfly fluttered down and kissed its petals. It was a suitor, but the rose let him fly away. Then a tremendously big grasshopper came, seated himself on a rose nearby, and rubbed his shins. Strangely enough, among grasshoppers, this is a token of affection.

The rose on which he perched did not understand it that way, but the one with the green crippled leaf did, for the big grasshopper looked at her with eyes that clearly meant, "I love you so much I could eat you." Surely this is as far as love can go, when one becomes part of another. But the rose was not taken in, and flatly refused to become one with this jumping fop. Then, in the starlit night a nightingale sang.

"He is singing just for me," said the rose with the blemish, or with the mark of distinction as she considered it. "Why am I so honored, above all my sisters? Why was I given this peculiarity—which makes me the luckiest one?"

Next to appear in the garden were two gentlemen, smoking their cigars. They spoke about roses and about tobacco. Roses, they say, are not supposed to stand tobacco smoke; it fades them and turns them green. This was to be tested, but the gentlemen would not take it upon themselves to try it out on the more perfect roses.

They tried it on the one with the defect.

"Ah ha! A new honor," the rose said. "I am lucky indeed—the luckiest of all." And she turned green with conceit and tobacco smoke.

One rose, little more than a bud but perhaps the loveliest one on the bush, was chosen by the gardener for the place of honor in an artistically tied bouquet. It was taken to the proud young heir of the household and rode beside him in his coach. Among other fragrant flowers and beautiful green leaves it sat in all its glory, sharing in the splendor of the festivities. Gentlemen and ladies, superbly dressed, sat there in the light of a thousand lamps as the music played. The theater was so brilliantly illuminated that it seemed a sea of light. Through it swept a storm of applause as a young dancer came upon the stage. One bouquet after another showered down, in a rain of flowers at her feet.

There fell the bouquet in which the lovely rose was set like a precious stone. The happiness it felt was complete, beyond any description. It felt all the honor and splendor around it, and as it touched the floor it fell to dancing too. The rose jumped for joy. It bounded across the stage at such a rate that it broke from its stem. The flower never came into the hands of the dancer. It rolled rapidly into the wings, where a stagehand picked it up. He saw how lovely and fragrant the rose was, but it had no stem. He pocketed it, and when he got home he put it in a wine glass filled with water. There the flower lay throughout the night, and early next morning it was placed beside his grandmother. Feeble and old, she sat in her easy chair and gazed at the lovely stemless rose that delighted her with its fragrance.

"You did not come to the fine table of a lady of fashion," she said.

"You came to a poor old woman. But to me you are like a whole rosebush. How lovely you are." Happy as a child, she gazed at the flower, and perhaps recalled the days of her own blooming youth that now had faded away.

"The window pane was cracked," said the Wind. "I got in without any trouble. I saw the old woman's eyes as bright as youth itself, and I saw the stemless but beautiful rose in the wine glass. Oh, it was the happiest of them all! I knew it! I could tell!"

Every rose on that bush in the garden had its own story. Each rose was convinced that it was the happiest one, and it is faith that makes us happy. But the last rose knew indeed that it was the happiest.

"I have outlasted them all," it said. "I am the last rose, the only one left, my mother's most cherished child!"

"And I am the mother of them all," the Rosebush said.

"No, I am," said the Sunshine.

"And I," said the Dew.

"Each had a share in it," the Wind at last decided, "and each shall have a part of it." And then the Wind swept its leaves out over the hedge where the dew had fallen, and where the sun was shining.

"I have my share too," said the Wind. "I have the story of all the roses, and I shall spread it throughout the wide world. Tell me then, which was the happiest of them all? Yes, that you must tell, for I have said enough."

THE DAYS OF THE WEEK (1868)

The days of the week once wanted to be free to get together and have a party. But each of the seven days was so occupied, the year around, that they had no time to spare. They wanted a whole extra day; but then they had that every four years, the intercalary day that comes in February for the purpose of keeping order in chronology.

On the intercalary day they would get together for a party, and, as February is the month of carnivals, they would come in costumes of each one's taste and choice; they would eat well, drink well, make speeches, and be complimentary and disagreeable to one another in unrestrained comradeship. While the Vikings of olden times used to throw their gnawed-off bones at each other's heads during mealtime, the days of the week intended to throw jokes and sarcastic witticisms such as might be in keeping with the innocent carnival spirit.

So when it was intercalary day, they assembled.

Sunday, foreman of the days of the week, appeared in a black silk cloak; pious people thought he was dressed for church in a minister's gown, but the worldly minded saw that he was attired in a domino for merriment and that the flashing carnation he wore in his buttonhole was a little red theater lantern on which it said, "All sold out; see now that you enjoy yourselves!"

Monday, a young fellow related to Sunday, and very fond of pleasures, came next. He left his workshop, he said, whenever he heard the music of the parade of the guard.

"I must go out and listen to Offenbach's music; it doesn't go to my head or to my heart; it tickles my leg muscles; I must dance, have a few drinks, get a black eye, sleep it off, and then the next day go to work. I am the new part of the week!"

Tuesday is Tyr's day, the day of strength.

"Yes, that I am," said Tuesday. "I take a firm grip on my work; I fasten Mercury's wings onto the merchant's boots, see that the wheels in the factory are oiled and turning, that the tailor sits at his table, and that the street paver is by his paving stones; each attends to his business, for I keep my eye on all. Accordingly, I am here in a police uniform and call myself Tuesday, a well-used day! If this is a bad joke, then you others try to think of a better one!"

"Then I come," said Wednesday. "I'm in the middle of the week. The Germans call me Herr Mittwoch. I stand like a journeyman in a store and like a flower in the midst of the other esteemed days of the week! If we all march up in order, then I have three days before me and three days behind; they are like an honor guard, so I should think that I am the most prominent day in the week!"

Thursday appeared dressed as a coppersmith, with a hammer and a copper kettle, as a symbol of his noble descent.

"I am of the highest birth," he said, "paganish, godlike! In the northern countries I am named after Thor, and in the southern countries after Jupiter, who both knew how to thunder and lighten, and that has remained in the family!"

And then he beat his copper kettle, thereby proving his high birth.

Friday was dressed as a young girl and called herself Freia, also Venus for a change, depending upon the language of the country in which she appeared. She was of a quiet, cheerful character, she said, but today she felt gay and free, for this was intercalary day, which, according to an old custom, gives a woman the right to dare propose to a man and not have to wait for him to propose to her.

Saturday appeared as an old housekeeper with a broom and other cleaning articles. Her favorite dish was beer soup, though at this festive occasion she did not request that it be served for everyone, only that she get it, and she got it.

And so the days of the week had their party.

Here they are in print, all seven of them, ready for use as tableaux at family parties. There you can make them as funny as you wish; we give them here as a joke on February, the only month with an extra day.

PIETER, PETER, AND PEER (1868)

It is unbelievable all that children know nowadays; one can scarcely say what they don't know. They no longer believe the old story that the stork brought them to father and mother out of the well or the millpond when they were little, and yet it is really true.

But how did the little ones get down into the millpond or the well? Ah, not everyone knows that, but there are some who do. Have you ever gazed at the sky on a clear, starry night and watched the many shooting stars? It is as if the stars fall from and disappear into nowhere. Even the most learned persons can't explain what they don't know themselves; but one can explain this when he knows it. It is like a little Christmas-tree candle that falls from heaven and is blown out. It is a soul spark from our Lord that flies toward the earth, and when it reaches our thick, heavy air, it loses its brilliancy, becoming something that our eyes cannot see, something much finer than air itself; it is a little child from heaven, a little angel, but without wings, for it is to become a human child.

Softly it glides through the air, and the wind carries it into a flower, which may be an orchid, a dandelion, a rose, or a cowslip, and there it lies and rests itself. And so light and airy is it that a fly can carry it off, as, of course, a bee can, when they alternately come to seek the sweetness of the flower. If the little air child lies in their way, they do not brush it aside. That they wouldn't have the heart to do! They take it and lay it under the leaf of a water lily in the sunshine, and from there it crawls and creeps into the water, where it sleeps and grows until it is large enough for the stork to see and bring to a human family that has been longing for a sweet little child. But whether it becomes sweet or not depends on whether it has drunk pure clean water or has swallowed mud and duckweed the wrong way; that makes one so filthy!

The stork, always without preference, takes the first one he sees. One goes to kind and loving parents in a fine home; another comes to unpleasant people in such misery that it would have been much better for it to have remained in the millpond.

The little ones can never remember afterward what they dreamed while they were lying under the water-lily leaf, listening to the frogs in the evening singing, "Coax! Coax! Coax!" In human language that means, "Now you go to sleep and dream!" Nor can they remember the flower where they first lay, nor how it smelled; and yet there is always something inside them, even when they are grown people, which makes them say, "I like this flower the best." That's because it is the one in which they were placed when they were air children.

The stork lives to be a very old bird, and he always has interest in the little ones he has brought and watches how they get along in the world and how they behave themselves. Of course, he can't do much for them or change anything in their lives, for he has his own family to look after, but at least he never lets them get out of his thoughts.

I know a very worthy, honest old stork who has had a great deal of experience, and has brought many little ones out of the water, and knows their stories—in which there is always a little mud and duckweed from the millpond. I begged him to tell me the story of one of them, and he said I should have three instead of one, and all from the Pietersens' house.

The Pietersens were an extremely nice family; the father was one of the thirty-two members of the town council, and that was an honor; he was completely wrapped up in his work with the thirty-two councilmen. When the stork brought a little fellow to this home he was named Peiter; the next year the stork brought another, and they named him Peter, and when the third one came they called him Peer—for all three names—Peiter, Peter, and Peer—are parts of the name Pietersen. So there were three brothers here—three shooting stars—and each had been cradled in a flower, then laid under the water-lily leaf in the millpond, and brought from there by the stork to the Pietersen family, whose house is on the corner, as you surely know.

They grew in body and mind, and wanted to become something more than the thirty-two councilmen were. Peiter had decided he wanted to be a robber; he had just seen the play Fra Diavolo, and that had convinced him that a robber's life was the most delightful in the world. Peter wanted to be a trash collector. And Peer, who was such a sweet and good boy, round and plump, whose only fault was biting his nails, wanted to be "Papa." That was what each of them said he was going to be in life, whenever anybody asked them about it.

Then they went to school. One was at the head of the class, and one at the foot, and one in the middle, but in spite of that they could be equally good and clever, and they were, said their very clearsighted parents. The three went to children's parties; they smoked when nobody was watching. They gained knowledge and made acquaintances.

From the time he was quite small, Peiter was quarrelsome,

just the way a robber ought to be. He was a very naughty boy, but his mother said that came from worms—naughty children always have worms—or from mud in the stomach. And one day his mother's new silk dress suffered from his obstinacy and naughtiness.

"Don't push the tea table, my good little lamb," she had said. "You might tip over the cream pitcher, and then I'd get spots on my new silk dress."

And so the "good little lamb" firmly took up the cream pitcher and firmly poured all the cream right into Mamma's lap. Mamma couldn't help saying, "Oh, lamb, lamb, that was careless of you, lamb!" But she had to admit that the child had a will of his own. A will means character, and that's very promising to a mother.

He might, of course, have become a robber, but he didn't, in the actual sense of the word; he only came to look like one, with his slouch hat, bare throat, and long, lank hair. He was supposed to be an artist, but he only got as far as the clothes. He looked like a hollyhock, and all the people he made drawings of looked like hollyhocks, so lanky were they. He was very fond of hollyhocks, and the stork said he had lain in that flower when he was an air child.

Peter must have lain in a buttercup. He looked buttery around the corners of his mouth, and his skin was so yellow that one would think that if his cheek were cut, butter would ooze out. He should have been a butter dealer, and could have been his own signboard; but on the inside he was a trash collector with a rattle. He was a musician of the Pietersen family—"musical enough for all of them," the neighbors said. He composed seventeen new polkas in one week, and then put them all together and made an opera out of them, with a trumpet and rattle accompaniment. Ugh! How delightful that was!

Peer was white and red, small and quite ordinary; he had lain in a daisy. He never hit back when the other boys beat him up; he said he was the most sensible, and the most sensible always gives way first.

He was a collector, first of slate pencils, and later of letter seals. Then he got a little cabinet of curiosities of natural history, in which were the skeleton of a stickleback, three blind baby rats preserved in alcohol, and a stuffed mole. Peer had a keen appreciation of science and an eye for the beauties of nature, and that was a comfort to his parents and to him, too. He preferred wandering in the woods to going to school, preferred nature to education.

Both his brothers were engaged to be married, but he could think of nothing but completing his collection of water-bird eggs. He knew much more about animals than he did about human beings; he even thought we could never reach the heights of the animals in the feeling we consider the loftiest of all—love. He saw that when the female nightingale was setting on the nest, Papa Nightingale would perch on a branch close by and sing to his little wife all night, "Kluk-kluk! Zi-Zi! Lo-lo-li!" Peer knew he could never do that or even think of doing such a thing. When Mamma Stork had her babies in the nest, Father Stork stood guard on the edge of the roof all night, on one leg. Peer couldn't have stood that way for an hour!

Then one day when he examined a spider's web, and saw what was in it, he gave up completely any idea of marriage. Mr. Spider weaves his web for catching thoughtless flies, old and young, fat and lean; he lives only to weave and to support his family. But Madam Spider lives only for him. Out of sheer love she eats him up; she eats his heart, his head, his stomach, until only his long thin legs are left in the web where he used to sit, anxious for the welfare of his family. Now that's the real truth, right out of the natural-history book! When Peer saw all this he grew very thoughtful; to be so dearly loved by a wife that she eats one up out of violent love? No! No human being could love like that, and would it be desirable, anyway?

Peer resolved never to marry, or even to give or take a kiss, for that might seem the first step toward marriage. But he did receive a kiss, anyway, the same kiss we all get someday, the great kiss of Death. When we have lived long enough, Death is given the order, "kiss him away," and so away the human goes. A ray of sunshine comes straight from our Lord, so bright that it almost blinds one. Then the soul that came from heaven as a shooting star goes back like a shooting star, but this time not to sleep in a flower or dream beneath the leaf of the water lily; it has more important things than that to do. It enters the great land of eternity; but what that is like and what it looks like there, no one can say. No one has looked into it, not even the stork, though he sees far and knows much.

The stork knew nothing more of Peer, whereas he could have told me lots more about Peiter and Peter. But I had heard enough of them, and I suppose you have, too, so I thanked him and bade him good-bye for this time. But now he demands three frogs and a little snake as payment for this simple little story—you see, he takes his pay in food. Will you pay him? I can't; I have neither frogs nor snakes.

THE COURT CARDS (1869)

Oh, so many dainty things can be cut out of pasteboard and pasted together! In this fashion there was cut and pasted a castle so large that it took up a whole tabletop, and it was painted so that it seemed to be built out of red brick. It had a shining copper roof; it had towers and a drawbridge; the water in the canals looked like plate glass, which is just what it was; and in the topmost tower there stood a watchman cut out of wood. He had a trumpet, but he didn't blow it.

All this belonged to a little boy named William. He raised and then lowered the drawbridge himself, and made his tin soldiers march over it. He opened the castle gate to peep into the spacious reception hall, where all the face cards from a pack—Hearts, Diamonds, Clubs and Spades—hung in frames upon the wall, like portraits in a real reception hall. The Kings each held a scepter and wore a crown. The Queens wore flowing veils over their shoulders, and in their hands each held a flower or a fan. The Knaves had halberds and nodding plumes.

One evening the little boy peered through the open gates of the castle to have a look at the Court Cards in the reception hall. It seemed to him that the Kings saluted him with their scepters, the Queen of Spades waved the golden tulip she held, the Queen of Hearts raised her fan, and all four Queens graciously took notice of him. As he came a little closer to get a better view, his head struck against the castle and shook it. Then the four Knaves, of Hearts, Diamonds, Clubs, and Spades, lifted their halberds to warn him not to try to press his way through.

The little boy understood, and gave them a friendly nod. He nodded again, and then he said: "Say something," but the Court Cards said not a word. However, when he nodded a third time to the Knave of Hearts, the Knave jumped out of his card and placed himself in the middle of the floor.

"What's your name?" he asked the youngster. "You have bright eyes and good teeth, but you don't wash your hands often enough." This was not a very polite way to talk.

"My name is William," said the youngster. "This castle is mine, and you are my Knave of Hearts."

"I'm my King's and my Queen's Knave, not yours," said the Knave of Hearts. "I can get off of the card and out of the frame too. So can my gracious King and Queen, even more easily than I. We can march right out into the wide world, but that's such a tiresome journey, and we have grown weary of it. It's more convenient, and more pleasant for us to be sitting in the cards, just being ourselves."

"Were all of you really human beings once?" asked the youngster.

"Human beings?" the Knave of Hearts said. "Yes, but we were not as good as we should have been. Now please light a little wax candle for me. I'd like a red one best, for red is the color of my King and Queen. Then I shall tell our whole story to the lord of the castle—I believe you said you were lord of the castle, didn't you? But don't interrupt me. If I speak, there must not be the slightest interruption.

"Do you see my King—the King of Hearts? Of these four Kings, he is the oldest, the first-born. He was born with a golden crown and a golden apple, and he began to rule immediately. His Queen was born with a golden fan. She still has it. They had a wonderful time, even in childhood. They did not have to go to school. They could amuse themselves all day long, building up castles and knocking them down, setting up tin soldiers, and playing with dolls. If they asked for a slice of bread and butter, their bread was buttered on both sides and nicely sprinkled with brown sugar too. This was in the good old days which were called the golden age, but they tired of it all, and so did I. Yes, those were the good old days!—and then the King of Diamonds took over the government."

The Knave didn't say any more. The little boy waited to hear something else, but not a syllable was spoken, so after a while he asked, "What then?"

The Knave of Hearts made him no answer. He stood erect and silent, with his eyes fixed on the burning wax candle. The youngster nodded, and nodded again, but he got not response. He then turned to the Knave of Diamonds, and when he had nodded to him three times the Knave leaped from the card to the center of the floor. He said only two words: "Wax candle!"

Understanding what he wanted, little William at once lighted a red candle and placed it before him. The Knave of Diamonds presented arms with his halberd, and said:

"Then the King of Diamonds came to the throne—a King with a pane of glass in his chest. The Queen also had a pane of glass in her chest, so people could look right inside them, though in all other respects they were shaped as normal human beings. They were so pleasant that a monument was raised in their honor. It stood without falling for seven whole years, but it was built to stand forever." The Knave of Diamonds presented arms and stared at the red wax candle.

Immediately, without any nod of encouragement from little William, the Knave of Clubs stepped down, as serious as the stork that strides with such dignity across the meadow. Like a bird, the black three-leafed clover in the corner of the card flew past the Knave and back again, to fit itself where it had fitted before. Without waiting for his wax candle—as the other knaves had done—the Knave of Clubs said:

"Not everyone gets his bread buttered on both sides and powdered with sugar. My King and Queen had none of that. They were compelled to go to school and learn what they had not learned before. They too had panes of glass in their chests, but nobody looked through the glass except to see if something was wrong with their works inside, and if possible to find out some reason for scolding them. I know it. I have served my King and Queen all my life long. I know all about them, and I obey all their orders. They commanded me to say nothing more tonight, so I keep silence and present arms."

But William lighted a candle for this Knave too—a candle, white as snow. Quickly—even more quickly than the candle was lighted—the Knave of Spades appeared in the center of the hall. He hurried along, yet he limped as if he had a lame leg. It creaked and cracked as if it had once been broken. Yes, he had met with many ups and downs in his life. Now he spoke:

"Yes, you have each got a candle, and I shall get one too. I know that. But if we Knaves are honored so highly, our Kings and Queens should have triple honors. And it is right that My King and Queen should have four candles each. Their story and trials are so sad and unhappy that they have good reason to dress in mourning and to wear a gravedigger's spade on their coat of arms. Poor Knave that I am, in one game of cards I have been nicknamed 'Black Peter.' Yes! but I have a name that isn't even fit to mention." So he whispered, "In another game I am nicknamed 'Dirty Mads'—I who was once first cavalier to the King of Spades. Now I am last! The history of my royal master and mistress I will not tell, for they do not wish me to do so. The little lord of the castle may imagine their story for himself if he will, but it is a most melancholy one. They have sunk pretty low, and their fate is not apt to change for the better until we all go riding on the red horse, higher than there are clouds."

And little William proceeded to light three candles apiece for the Kings, and three for the Queens. But for the King and Queen of Spades, he lighted four candles apiece, and the whole reception hall became as dazzlingly bright as the wealthiest emperor's palace. The four Kings and Queens made each other serene bows and gracious curtsies. The Queen of Hearts fluttered her golden fan, and the Queen of Spades twirled her golden tulip in a wheel of fire. The royal couples came down from their cards and frames to move in a graceful minuet across the floor. They were dancing in and out among the candle flames, and the Knaves were dancing too.

Suddenly the entire reception hall was ablaze. The fire roared up through the windows and the walls, and everything was a curtain of flames that crackled and hissed. The whole castle was wrapped in fire and smoke. William was frightened. He ran shouting to his father and mother, "Fire, fire! My castle's on fire!" It sparkled and blazed, but from the flames it sang:

"Now we are riding the red horse, higher than the clouds.

This is the way it behooves Kings and Queens to go. And this is the way it behooves their Knaves to follow."

Yes! That was the end of William's castle, and of the Court Cards. William is still alive, and he washes his hands. It was not his fault that the castle burned.

LUCK MAY LIE IN A PIN (1869)

A STORY TOLD FOR MY YOUNG AMERICAN FRIENDS

I'll tell you a story about luck. All of us know what it is to be lucky. Some know good luck day in, day out; others only now and then in their lucky seasons; and there are some people who know it only once in a lifetime. But luck comes at some time or other to us all.

Now I needn't tell you what everyone knows, that it's God who puts little children in their mother's lap; maybe in a nobleman's castle, maybe in a workingman's home, or maybe in the open field where the cold wind blows. What you may not know, though it's just as true, is that when God leaves the child he always leaves it a lucky piece. He doesn't put this where the child is born, but tucks it away in some odd corner of the Earth where we least expect it. Yes, you can rest assured that it always turns up, sooner or later, and that is nice to know.

This lucky piece may turn out to be an apple. That was the case with one man, a scholar called Newton. The apple fell into his lap, and his luck came with it. If you don't know the story, get someone to tell it to you. I've a different story to tell, about a pear.

Once there was a man born poor, bred poor, and married without a penny. By the way, he was a turner by trade, but as he made nothing except umbrella handles and umbrella rings, he earned only enough money to live from hand to mouth.

"I'll never find my luck," he used to say.

Now this is a gospel true story. It really happened. I could name the man's county and his town, but that isn't important. Wild service berries, with their red, sour fruit, grew around his house and garden as if they were the richest ornament. However, in the garden was also a pear tree. It had never borne fruit; yet the man's luck lay hidden in the tree, in the shape of a pear not yet to be seen.

One night the wind blew in a terrible gale. In the next town men said that the great mail coach was lifted from one side of the road to the other as easily as a rag, so it was not to be wondered at that a large branch was torn from the pear tree. The branch was brought into the workshop and, just as a joke, the turner made from it wooden pears, big, little, and middle-sized.

"For once my tree has borne pears," he smiled, and gave them to his children for playthings.

Among the necessities of life are umbrellas, especially in lands where it rains a lot. But the turner's family had only one umbrella between them. When the wind blew hard, their umbrella would blow inside out. Sometimes it would break, and luckily the man knew how to mend it. However, with the button and loop that held the umbrella closed, things went from bad to worse. The button would always fly off just as they thought they had the umbrella neatly folded.

One day it popped off, and the turner hunted for it everywhere. In a crack of the floor he came across one of the smallest pears he had given his children for a toy.

"If I can't find the button," he said, "I'll make this do." He fitted a string through it, and the little pear buttoned up the umbrella to perfection. It was the best umbrella fastener that ever was seen.

The next time the turner sent umbrella handles and umbrella rings to the city, he added several of the small wooden pears. They were fitted to a few new umbrellas, and put with a thousand others on a ship bound for America. Americans catch on very quickly. They saw that the little pears held better than the other umbrella buttons, and the merchant gave orders that all the umbrellas sent to him henceforth should be fastened with little wooden pears.

There was work for you—thousands of pears to be made for all the umbrellas that went to America. The turner turned them out wholesale, until the whole pear tree was used up making little wooden pears. They brought pennies that grew into dollars. There was no end to the money he made.

"My luck was in that pear tree all along," the man said. Soon he had a great factory with plenty of workmen to help him. Now that he always had time for a joke he would say, "Good luck may lie in a pin."

And I who tell this story say so too, for it's a true proverb in Denmark that if you put a white pin in your mouth you'll be invisible. But it must be the right sort of pin, a lucky piece from God's own hand. I have one of them, and whenever I come to America, that new world so far away and yet so near me, I'll always carry that pin. Already my words have gone there. The ocean rolls toward America, and the wind blows that way. Any day I can be where my stories are read, and perhaps see the glitter of ringing gold—the gold that is best of all, which shines in children's eyes, or rings from their lips and the lips of their grown-ups. I am in all my friends' homes, even though they don't see me. I have the white pin in my mouth.

And luck may lie in a pin.

SUNSHINE STORIES (1869)

I'll tell you a story," said the Wind. "Kindly remember," said the Rain, "that it's my turn to talk. You've been howling around the corner at the top of your voice quite long enough."

"Is that the thanks I get for all of the favors I've done you?" the Wind blustered. "Many an umbrella I've turned inside out, or even blown to tatters, when people tried to avoid you."

"Be silent! It is I who shall speak," said the Sunshine, who spoke with such brilliance and warmth that the weary Wind fell flat on his back, and the Rain shook him and tried to rouse him, crying: "We won't stand for it. This Madam Sunshine is forever interrupting us. Don't let's listen to her. What she says is not worth hearing."

And the Sunshine began: "A beautiful swan flew over the rolling, tossing waves of the ocean. Each of its feathers shone like gold. One feather drifted down above a great merchant ship that sailed the sea with all its canvas spread. The feather came to rest upon the curly hair of a young overseer who looked after the goods aboard that ship—"supercargo," they called him. The bird of fortune's feather touched his forehead, became a quill pen in his hand, and brought him such luck that he soon became a merchant, a man of wealth, a man so rich that he could wear spurs of gold and change a golden dish into a nobleman's shield. I know—I have shone on it," said the Sunshine.

"The swan flew far away, over a green meadow where a little

shepherd boy, not more than seven years old, lay in the shade of an old tree, the only tree in that meadow. As the swan flew past it, she brushed one leaf from the tree. This leaf fell into the boy's hands, where it turned into three leaves, ten leaves—yes, it turned into all the leaves of a book. In this book he read of the many wonderful things that are in nature, about his native language, about faith, and about knowledge. Before he went to sleep he laid the book under his pillow to keep from forgetting what he had learned during the day. The wonderful book led him first to school, and then far into the fields of learning. I have seen his name where they carve the names of great scholars," the Sunshine said.

"The swan flew over the forest, where it was lonely and quiet. She came to rest on a deep blue lake, where the water lilies grow, where wild apple trees flourish along the shore, and where the cuckoo and wild pigeon make their nests.

"A poor woman was in the forest, gathering fallen branches. She carried them on her back, and held a baby in her arms. She saw the golden swan, that bird of fortune, rise from the rush-covered shore. What was this glittering thing the swan had left? It was a golden egg, still warm. She put it in her bosom, and the warmth stayed in it. Truly there was life in that egg. Yes, she heard a tapping inside the shell, but it was so faint that she mistook it for the sound of her own heartbeat.

"When she came home to her own poor cottage, she took the egg out to look at it. 'Tick,' it said, 'tick,' as if it had been a costly gold watch. But it was no watch. It was an egg, just about to hatch. The shell cracked open, and a dear little baby swan looked out. It was fully feathered, all in gold, and around its neck were four gold rings. As the poor woman had four boys—three at home and the baby she had carried in her arms—she knew that one of the rings was meant for each of her sons. As soon as she realized this, the little golden bird flew away. She kissed all of the rings, and she made each son kiss one of them, touch it against his heart, and wear it on his finger. I saw all this," said the Sunshine, "and I saw what came of it.

"As one of the boys played in the bed of a stream, he picked up a handful of clay. He turned it, and twisted it, and he shaped it in his fingers until he had made a statue of Jason. Like Jason, the young sculptor had found the golden fleece he sought.

"The second boy ran across the meadow, where there were flowers of every hue. He gathered a handful, and squeezed them so tightly that the colored juices wet his ring and splashed in his eye. They stuck to his fingers and colored his thoughts. The days went by, and the years went past, until people in the big city came to speak of him as 'the great painter.'

"The third boy clenched his ring in his teeth so tightly that it echoed the song that lay deep in his heart. The things he thought and the things he felt were turned to music. The rose like singing swans, and like swans they plunged down as deep as the depths of the sea, 'the Deep Sea of Thoughts.' He became a great musician, a great composer of whom every land has the right to say: 'He belongs to me.'

"The fourth boy—the baby—was an outcast. They said he had the pip, and that like a sick little chicken he should be dosed with butter and pepper. They gave him pepper enough with his butter, but I gave him warmth and the kiss of the sun," said the Sunshine. "He got ten kisses for one that the other children received. He was a poet, who met with a blow and a kiss, all his life long. But he had something that no one could take from him. He had the ring of fame from the golden swan of fortune. There were golden wings to his thoughts. Up they flew and away they went, like golden butterflies, which are the symbol of things immortal."

"What an extremely long story," said the Wind. "And so awfully dull," the Rain agreed. "Fan me, if you please, so I may revive a little." The Wind blew again, and the Sunshine said: "The swan of fortune flew over the deep gulf, where fishermen spread their nets. The poorest of the fishermen thought of getting married, and marry he did. And to him the swan brought a lump of amber. Amber has the power to draw things to it, and it drew the hearts to the fisherman's home. Amber makes the most wonderful incense, and there came a fragrant air as from a church, like a balmy breeze from God's nature. So the fisherman and his bride were happy and thankful in their quiet home. They were content with what little they had, and their life became a complete sunshine story."

"I think," said the Wind, "that these stories should stop. The Sunshine has talked long enough, and I am very bored."

"So am I," said the Rain.

And what do we others who knew this story say?

We say: "Now it's out."

WHAT ONE CAN INVENT (1869)

There was once a young man who studied to become a poet. He wanted to be a poet by next Easter, so that he could marry and earn his living from poetry, which he knew was just a matter of making things up. But he had no imagination. He firmly believed he had been born too late. Every subject had been used up before he had a chance at it, and there was nothing in the world left to write about.

"How happy were the people born a thousand years ago," he sighed. "Then it was an easy thing to be immortal. Even those who were born a hundred years ago were lucky compared with me. They still had things left to make poems about. But now every subject is worn out, and it's no use for me to try my pen on such threadbare stuff."

He thought about it, and worried about it, until he grew very thin and woebegone, the poor fellow. No doctor could help him, but there was one person who would know just the remedy he needed to set him right. She was a little old lady, wonderfully wise, who lived in a tiny gatehouse in the turnpike. She opened and closed the toll gate for everyone who rode by, but she was learned in the ways of the world. She was a clever woman who could do more than open a gate, and she knew far more than the doctor who drives in his own carriage and pays taxes.

"I must go to her," the young man said. He found her house small and tidy, but most uninteresting. Not a tree, not a flower, grew anywhere near it. There was a beehive by her door—very useful; there was a potato patch—very useful; and over the ditch a blackthorn bush had flowered, and now bore fruit—very sour berries that puckered your mouth if you tasted them before they were ripened by frost.

The young man thought to himself, "What a perfect picture this is of the commonplace times we live in." But at least it had set him thinking. He had found the flash of an idea at the old lady's doorway.

"Write it down," she told him. "Crumbs are the same stuff that bread is made of. I know why you have come. You have no imagination, but you want to be a poet by Easter."

"Everything has been written before I was born," he sighed. "Our times are not like the old days."

"Indeed they aren't," the little old lady agreed. "In the old days women like me, who knew dark secrets and how to cure by the use of strange herbs, were burned alive. In the old days poets went about with empty stomachs, and their clothes ragged and patched. Ours are excellent times, the best times of all. But your lack of imagination comes from not using your eyes, and not using your ears, and not saying your prayers at night. There are things all around you to write about, if you only knew how. You can find poetry in the earth, where it grows and flourishes. Whether you dip into the water of a running stream or a stagnant pool, you will find poetry. But first you must understand how to find it. You must learn how to catch the sunlight as it falls. Just try on my spectacles, listen through my ear trumpet, say your prayers, and please, for once in your life, stop thinking about yourself."

That last request was asking almost too much of him. It was

more than any woman, however wise and wonderful, should demand of a poet.

When he put on her spectacles and ear trumpet, she turned him out into the potato patch, where she gave him a large potato to hold in his hands.

What did the potato find to tell him about? It told about itself and its forefathers, about the coming of the potato to Europe; about how unjustly it was suspected and abused before anyone realized that potatoes were far more valuable than any lump of gold.

"By the king's own order, we were distributed from the town hall of each city and village. A manifesto was issued to proclaim our great value and merits, but nobody believed it. No one had the least notion of how to plant us. One man dug a hole and emptied his whole bushel of potatoes in it. Another stuck them in the ground, far apart from each other, and waited for the potatoes to grow into trees, so one could shake them off the branches. They saw us grow buds and flowers and watery fruit, but it all withered away. No one thought to look for our real fruit, the potatoes that lay out of sight in the ground. Ah yes, we suffered many abuses—at least our forefathers did—but it was all for the best. Now you know our story."

"That will do," the old lady said. "Come and look at the blackthorn bush."

"We, too," said the blackthorn, "have many relations in the land from which the potatoes came, further north than where they grew. A party of bold Norsemen steered westerly from Norway through fogs and storms, till they came to an unknown land. Here, buried under snow and ice, they found grass and shrubs, and a bush with dark blue berries like the grapes that grow on the vine. These were blackthorn berries that ripen in the frost, the same as ours, so the country was called 'Vineland,' or 'Greenland,' and sometimes 'Blackthorn Land.'"

"What a romantic story!" the young man said.

"Now follow me," the little old lady told him, and she led him to the beehive. It seethed with life. When he looked inside it he saw bees stationed in all the hallways, moving their wings like fans so that the air would be fresh in every part of this great honey mill. That was their business. Other bees came in from the sunshine and flowers. Those bees were born with baskets on their legs. They brought flower dust and emptied it out of their little leg-baskets, to be sorted and made into honey or wax. There was much going and coming. The queen of the hive wanted to try her wings, but when she flies all the other bees have to fly with her. Though the time for this swarming had not yet come, she was bent upon flight. So the bees bit off her majesty's wings to keep her from flying away, and she had to stay right where she belonged.

"Now climb to the top of the ditch, where you have a view of the high road," said the little old lady.

"My goodness! What swarms of people I see," said the young man. "What endless stories I seem to hear in all that buzzing, droning, and confusion. I feel dizzy! I shall fall!"

"Don't!" said the old lady. "Don't fall backward. Go straight forward, right in among the people. Have eyes for all you see, ears for all you hear, and above all throw your whole heart into it. Soon you will find that you do have imagination, and you'll have many thoughts to write down. But before you go, you must give back my spectacles and ear trumpet." She took them from him.

"Now I can't see anything," the young man said. "I can't even hear anything."

"In that case, you won't be a poet by Easter," the little old lady told him.

"Then when shall I be one?" he asked her.

"Neither by Easter, nor yet by Whitsuntide. You have no knack for imagination."

"But how then shall I ever make my living from poetry?"

"That you can do even before Lent. Write about those who write. To criticize their writing is to criticize them, but don't let that trouble you. The more critically you write, the more you'll earn, and you and your wife will eat cake every day."

"How she does imagine things," the young man thought, as he thanked her and said goodbye. But he did just as she told him. Since he could not be a poet himself—since he could not imagine—he took to writing criticism of all those who were poets. And he handled them with no light hand.

All this was told me by the little old lady who knows what one may imagine.

WHAT HAPPENED TO THE THISTLE (1869)

Adjoining the rich estate was a lovely and beautifully kept garden of rare trees and flowers. Guests at the estate enjoyed this fine garden and praised it. People from the countryside all round about and townspeople as well would come every Sunday and holiday to ask if they might see the garden. Even whole schools made excursions to it.

Just outside the fence that separated the garden from a country lane, there grew a very large thistle. It was so unusually big with such vigorous, full-foliaged branches rising from the root that it well deserved to be called a thistle bush. No one paid any attention to her except one old donkey that pulled the dairymaid's cart. He would stretch his old neck toward the thistle and say, "You're a beauty. I'd like to eat you!" But his tether was not long enough to let him reach the thistle and eat her.

There was a big party at the manor house. Among the guests were fine aristocratic relations from the capital—charming young girls, and among them was a young lady who had come from a foreign land, all the way from Scotland. Her family was old, and noble, and rich in lands and gold. She was a bride well worth winning, thought more than one young man, and their mothers thought so too.

The young people amused themselves on the lawn, where they played croquet. As they strolled about in the garden, each young lady plucked a flower and put in a young man's buttonhole. The young lady from Scotland looked all around her for a flower. But none of them suited her until she happened to look over the fence and saw the big, flourishing thistle bush, full of deep purple, healthy-looking flowers. When she saw them she smiled and asked the young heir of the household to pick one of them for her.

"That is Scotland's flower," she said. "It blooms on my country's coat of arms. That's the flower for me."

He plucked the best flower of the thistle, and pricked his finger in the process as much as if he had torn the blossom from the thorniest rosebush.

When she put it in his buttonhole, he considered it a great honor. Every other young man would gladly have given his lovely garden flower for any blossom from the slender fingers of the girl from Scotland. If the heir of the household felt himself highly honored, how much more so the thistle! She felt as full as if the sunshine and dew went through her.

"I must be more important than I thought," she said to herself. "I really belong inside, not outside the fence. One gets misplaced in the world, but I now have one of my offspring not only over the fence but actually in a buttonhole!"

To every one of her buds that bloomed, the thistle bush told what had happened. Not many days went by before she heard important news. She heard it not from passersby, nor from the chirping of little birds, but from the air itself, which collects sounds and carries them far and wide—from the shadiest walks of the garden and from the furthest rooms of the manor, where doors stood ajar and windows were left open. She heard that the young man who got the thistle flower from the slender fingers of the girl from Scotland now had won her heart and hand. They made a fine couple, and it was a good match.

"I brought that about," the thistle believed, thinking of how her flower had been chosen for the gentleman's buttonhole. Each new bud that opened was told of this wonderful happening.

"Undoubtedly I shall now be transplanted into the garden," thought the thistle. "Perhaps they will even pinch me into a flowerpot, which is the highest honor of all." She thought about this so long that at length she said with full and firm conviction, "I am to be planted in a flowerpot."

Every little thistle bud which opened was promised that it too would be put in a pot, perhaps even in a buttonhole, which was the highest it could hope to go. But not one of them reached a flowerpot, much less a buttonhole. They lived upon light and air. By day they drank sunshine, by night they drank dew, and were visited by bees and wasps who came in search of a dowry—the honey of the flower. And they took away the honey, but left the flowers behind.

"Such a gang of robbers!" said the thistle bush. "I'd like to stick a thorn through them, but I can't."

Her flowers faded and fell away, but new ones came in their place. "You have come as if you were called for," the thistle bush told them. "I expect to cross the fence any minute now."

A couple of innocent daisies and some tall, narrow-leaved canary grass listened with deepest admiration and believed everything that they heard. The old donkey, who had to pull the milk cart looked longingly at the blooming thistle bush and reached out for it, but his tether was too short.

The thistle thought so hard and so long about the Scotch thistle, whom she considered akin to her, that she began to believe that she herself had come from Scotland and that it was her own ancestors who had grown on the Scottish arms. This was toplofty thinking, but then tall thistles are apt to think tall thought.

"Sometimes one is of more illustrious ancestry than he ventures to suppose," said a nettle which grew nearby. It had a notion that it could be transformed into fine muslin if properly handled.

Summer went by, and fall went by, and the leaves fell from the trees. The flowers were more colorful, but less fragrant. On the other side of the fence the gardener's boy sang:

Up the hill and down the hill,
That's the way the world goes still.

And the young fir trees in the woods began to look forward to Christmas, though Christmas was a long time off.

"Here I still stay," said the thistle. "It is as if nobody thinks of me any more, yet it was I who made the match. They were engaged, and now they have been married. That was eight days ago. But I haven't progressed a single step—how can I?"

Several weeks went by. The thistle had one last, lonely flower. Large and full, it grew low, near the root. The cold wind blew over it, its color faded, its splendor departed. Only the thistle-shaped cup remained, as large as an artichoke blossom, and as silvery as a sunflower.

The young couple, who now were man and wife, came down the garden walk along the fence. The bride looked over the fence, and said, "Why, there still stands the big thistle, but it hasn't a flower left."

"Yes, there's the ghost of one—the very last one." Her husband pointed to the silvery shell of the flower—a flower itself.

"Isn't it lovely!" she said. "We must have one just like that carved around the frame of our picture."

Once again, the young man had to climb the fence and pluck the silvery shell of the thistle flower. It pricked his fingers well, because he had called it a ghost. Then it was brought into the garden, to the mansion, and to the parlor. There hung a large painting—The Newly Married Couple! In the groom's buttonhole, a thistle was painted. They spoke of that thistle flower, and they spoke of this thistle shell, this last silvered, shining flower of the thistle which they had brought in with them, and which was to be copied in the carving of the frame. The air carried their words about, far and wide.

"What strange things can happen to one," said the thistle. "My oldest child was put in a buttonhole, and my youngest in a picture frame. I wonder where I shall go."

The old donkey by the roadside looked long and lovingly at the thistle. "Come to me, my sweet," he said. "I cannot come to you because my tether is not long enough."

But the thistle did not answer. She grew more and more thoughtful, and she thought on right up to Christmastime, when this flower came of all her thinking:

"When one's children are safe inside, a mother may be content to stand outside the fence."

"That's a most honorable thought," said the sunbeam. "You too shall also have a good place."

"In a flowerpot or in a frame?" the thistle asked.

"In a fairy tale," said the sunbeam. And here it is.

CHICKEN GRETHE'S FAMILY (1869)

Chicken Grethe was the only human tenant of the fine new house that was built for the hens and ducks on the estate. It was built where the old baronial castle had stood with its tower, crow's-perch gable, moat, and drawbridge. Close by was a complete wilderness of trees and bushes. This had been the garden, running down to a big lake which was now a marsh. Rooks, crows, and jackdaws—a whole horde of screeching, cawing birds, hovered over the trees. The flock did not seem to diminish but rather to increase when one fired among them. They could be heard even inside the poultry house where Chicken Grethe sat with the ducklings waddling about her wooden shoes. She knew each chicken and every duck from the moment it hatched. She took pride in her chickens and her ducks, and in the fine house that had been built for them.

Her little room was clean and tidy. Her mistress, who owned the chicken house, insisted upon neatness, for she frequently brought distinguished visitors to see "the barracks of her hens and ducks," as she called the place.

She had a rocking chair, and a wardrobe, and even a chest of drawers, on which stood a highly polished brass plate with the name "Grubbe" engraved on it. This was the name of the old noble family that had lived there in the days when the castle was standing. The brass plate had been found while they were digging the ground and the parish clerk said that it had no value except as a relic. The clerk knew all about the place and the old days, for he was a scholar and his table drawer was filled with manuscripts. He knew much about the old days, but perhaps the oldest crow knew more and jabbered it out in his own language, but that was crow-talk, which the clerk did not understand, learned though he was.

Toward the end of a hot summer day, the mist would rise over the marsh until it looked as if there were a lake beyond the old trees where the rooks, crows, and jackdaws lived. This was how it had looked when old Sir Grubbe had lived there, and the castle with its massive red walls was still standing. In those days the dog's chain used to reach clear across the gateway. By way of the tower one came to the stone-flagged passage that led to the living quarters. The windows were narrow and the panes quite small, even in the great hall where they used to dance. But in the days of the last Grubbes, there had been no dancing for as far back as a man could remember, though an old kettledrum that had been used in the orchestra still remained in the hall. And there was also a curiously carved cupboard in which the rare flower bulbs were stored, for Lady Grubbe took pleasure in planting and in cultivating flowers and trees. Her husband preferred to hunt wild boars and wolves, and his little daughter, Marie, always rode with him. When she was no more than five years old, she sat proudly on horseback and gazed fearlessly about with her great dark eyes. She delighted in cracking her whip among the hounds, though her father would rather have seen her lash out among the peasant boys who came to stare at the gentry.

The peasant who lived in a clay hut near the castle had a son named Sören who was of the same age as the well-born little lady. He knew how to climb trees, and he had to bring bird nests down to her. The birds screamed as loud as they could scream, and one of the largest of them struck him so hard right above his eye that blood ran down, and they thought at first that he had lost an eye, but it had not been injured. Marie Grubbe called him "her Sören," a sign of high favor which once served to protect even his father, poor Jon. When he had done something wrong one day, Jon was condemned to ride the wooden horse. This contrivance stood in the yard, with four poles for legs, and for its back a single small rail which Jon had to straddle. Lest he ride it too comfortably, heavy bricks were tied to his feet. He made such agonized faces that little Sören wept and went down on his knees to beg Marie to have his father released. She instantly commanded that his father should be taken down. When she was not obeyed, Marie stamped her small feet on the flagstones and tugged at her father's coat sleeve until she tore it. She would have her way, and she got it. Sören's father was released.

Lady Grubbe came to her, stroked her hair, and looked at her daughter with mild, approving eyes. But Marie did not understand why. She would go with the hounds, not with her mother, who went down through the garden to the lake, where the water lilies bloomed, and where the bulrushes swayed among the reeds. "How charming," Lady Grubbe would say, as she admired this fresh, abundant growth. A then very rare tree, which she herself had planted, grew in her garden. A blood beech it was called, a sort of dark Moor among the other trees, so dark brown were its leaves. It needed plenty of sunlight, for in constant shade its leaves would turn green like those of other trees and thus lose their distinction. In her tall chestnut trees, in the shrubbery, and even the grass were many bird nests. The birds seemed to understand that they were safe here, where no one dared fire a gun.

But little Marie came here with Sören who, as we know, could climb, and she sent him to bring her down both the eggs and the downy little birds. The parent birds fluttered about in terror and anguish. Large and small—lapwings from the lawns, rooks, crows, and jackdaws from the tall trees—they screamed and shrieked just as their progeny shriek today.

"Children, what are you doing?" the gentlewoman cried. "What a wicked thing to do."

Sören looked ashamed and even the high-born young girl looked a little embarrassed, but then she said in an abrupt and sulky way: "My father lets me do this."

"Away, away!" the blackbirds shrieked, and away they flew, but they came back the next day because they lived there.

But the quiet gentlewoman did not live there much longer. The Lord called her away, and with him she was more at home than ever she was in this house. The church bells solemnly tolled as her body was carried to the church, and poor men's eyes grew dim, for she had shown them kindness. And now that she was gone no one looked after her plants, so the garden went to rack and ruin.

"Sir Grubbe is a hard man," people would say, "but young as she is, his daughter can handle him." He would laugh and let her have her will. She was twelve years old now, tall and well built. She looked right through people with her great dark eyes, rode her horse like a man, and shot her gun like an experienced hunter.

It came to pass that great men visited that district. They were as great as great can be—the young king with his half brother and crony, Lord Ulrick Frederick Gyldenlöve. They came to hunt wild boar, and they planned to stay overnight at Sir Grubbe's castle.

At the table, when Gyldenlöve sat beside Marie, he took her about the neck and gave her a kiss, just as if they had been related. But she gave him a slap in the face, and told him she could not stand him. This caused great laughter, as if it were a most pleasing sight.

And maybe it was, because five years later, when Marie was seventeen, Gyldenlöve sent a messenger with a letter asking for her hand in marriage. That was something!

"He is the highest and most gallant lord in the land," said Sir Grubbe. "You cannot refuse him."

"I don't like him much," Marie Grubbe said, but she did not turn down the highest lord in the land, who sat next to the king.

Her silver, woolens, and linens were sent by ship to Copenhagen. Marie made the trip overland in ten days, but the ship with the dowry met with contrary winds, or no wind at all. It took four months to reach Copenhagen, and when it did get there Lady Gyldenlöve had gone.

"I'd sooner lie on sacks than in his silken bed," she said. "I'd sooner walk barefoot than ride in a carriage with him."

Late on an evening in November, two women came riding into the town of Aarhus. They were Lady Gyldenlöve and her maid. They came from Veile, where they had arrived by ship from Copenhagen. They rode up to Sir Grubbe's town house. He was not at all pleased to see Marie. He gave her harsh words, but he did give her a bedroom. She got her beer broth for breakfast, but no good words to go with it. Her father's bad temper had turned against her, and she was not used to it. Her own temper was by no means mild. As one is spoken to, so one answers, and answer she did. Of her husband she spoke with bitterness and hatred. She declared that she could not live with him; she was too honorable and virtuous for that.

In this fashion a year went by, most unpleasantly. Bitter words passed between father and daughter. That should not be. Bitter words bear bitter fruit. What would be the outcome?

One day her father said, "We cannot live under the same roof. You must move to our old castle. I would rather you bit off your tongue than spoke lies."

So they parted. With her maid, she went to the old estate where she was born and bred, and where her mother, that pious gentlewoman, lay in the churchyard vault.

An old cowherd lived in the castle, and that was all. Cobwebs, heavy and black with dirt, draped every room. The garden was not taken care of. Wild hops and other climbing vines wove a tangled web between trees and shrubbery. Hemlock and nettles grew tall and rank. The blood beech had been outgrown, and in the deep shade, its leaves had turned as green as those of ordinary trees. Its glory was gone.

Rooks, crows, and jackdaws flew in enormous flocks above the tall chestnuts. They shrieked and cawed as if they had great news to tell each other. Here she was again, the girl who ordered their eggs and babies to be stolen from their nests. The real thief, the one who had actually stolen them, was now climbing a leafless tree. He clung to the tall ship's mast, and got his share of lashes with a rope's end if he didn't behave himself.

All this was told in our own time by the parish clerk. He had pieced it together from books and letters, and it lay with many another manuscript hidden away in his table drawer. "Up and down is the way the world goes," said he. "It's a curious story to hear." We want to hear how it went with Marie Grubbe, but we shall not lose track of Chicken Grethe who sat there in her fine hen house, in our own day. Marie Grubbe sat in this place in her day, but not so contentedly as old Chicken Grethe.

Winter went by. Spring and summer passed, and again came the stormy autumn with its cold and wet fog. It was a dull and dreary life there on the old estate. Marie Grubbe would snatch up her gun and go out on the heath to shoot hares or foxes and whatever birds she could find. More than once on these excursions she encountered a nobleman, Sir Palle Dyre from Nörrebaek, with his gun and his dogs. He was a big man who enjoyed boasting of his strength when he talked with her. He might have been a match for the departed Mr. Brockenhus of Egeskov, at Fyen, whom people still remember as a man of might. Like him, Palle Dyre had fastened a hunting horn to an iron chain over his gateway. When he came home he would catch hold of the chain, lift himself and his horse clear off the ground, and sound the horn.

"You must come to my castle and see that, Lady Marie," he said, "for we have fine fresh air at Nörrebaek." We have no record of when she went to Nörrebaek, but on the candlesticks at Nörrebaek church it is inscribed that they were given by Palle Dyre and Marie Grubbe of Nörrebaek Castle. Body and strength had Palle Dyre. He could drink like a sponge. He was like a cask that could never be filled. He snored enough for a whole pig pen, and he looked red and bloated.

"A cunning swine and a nagging fool he is," said Lady Palle

Dyre, the daughter of Grubbe. She soon grew weary of the life there, which did not improve matters. At dinnertime one day, the food got cold on the table. Palle Dyre was off fox hunting, and Lady Dyre could not be found. Palle Dyre came home at midnight. Lady Dyre came home neither by midnight nor by morning. She turned her back upon Nörrebaek, and rode away without a word of farewell. The weather was cloudy and wet. The wind was sharp, and the flock of blackbirds that croaked over her head were not as homeless as she.

First she rode south, almost to Germany. She turned a couple of gold rings with precious stones into ready money. She went east and she went west, with no fixed goal. She was angry with everybody and even with the good Lord himself, so sick was her mind. And soon her body was sick, too. She could scarcely drag her feet along. The lapwing flew up from its tuft of grass when she stumbled upon it and fell. The bird screamed, as it always does, "You thief, you thief!" Yet she had never stolen her neighbors' goods, except for the birds' eggs and nestlings taken from the clumps of grass and the tall trees when she was a little girl. She thought of that now.

From where she lay, she could see the sand dunes along the beach. Fishermen lived there, but she was too ill to crawl so far. The great white sea gulls came screaming over her as the rooks, crows, and jackdaws screamed above the trees at home. The birds flew nearer and nearer, until at last she thought they were blackbirds. But then everything went black before her eyes.

When she opened her eyes again she was being carried in the arms of a tall, strapping fellow. She looked straight into his bearded face and saw that he had a scar over one eye that appeared to divide the eyebrow in two. Sick as she was, he carried her to his ship, where he was abused by the shipmaster for bringing such a burden.

The ship set sail next day. Marie Grubbe sailed with it—she was not put ashore. Didn't she ever come back? Yes, but when and how?

The parish clerk could tell about this, too. It was not a tale which he had pieced together. He had the whole strange story from a reliable book which we can get and read for ourselves.

The Danish author, Ludvig Holberg, who has written so many books worth reading and so many gay comedies by which we get to know his time and its people, mentions Marie Grubbe in his letters, which tell how and in what part of the world he found her. This is well worth hearing, but we shall not lose track of Chicken Grethe, who sits so happy and comfortable in her imposing chicken house.

The ship sailed off with Marie Grubbe. That was where we left off. Year upon year went by.

The plague was raging in Copenhagen. That was in the year of 1711. The Queen of Denmark went to her German home. The king left his capital, and everyone who could made haste to leave. The students, even those who had free board and lodging, scurried out of the city. One of them, the last student left at what they called Borch's College, near the students' headquarters, made ready to go. At two o'clock in the morning he started out, with his knapsack stuffed with more books and manuscripts than clothes. A raw, dank mist hung over the city. Not a soul was to be seen in the street through which he passed. All around him the gates and doors were marked with the crosses which showed that there people lay ill or had died of the plague. Even in broad and winding Meatmonger's street—as the street leading from the round tower to the king's palace was called then—there was not a man to be seen. Suddenly a large hearse came rumbling by. The driver cracked his whip to urge his horses into a gallop, for the wagon was crammed with corpses. The young student covered his face with his hands, and breathed the fumes of strong spirits which he carried in a brass-boxed sponge.

From a grog shop in one of the streets came the sound of songs and forced laughter. Men were drinking the night away in an effort to forget that Death stood at their door, beckoning to them to come with him and join the other dead men in the hearse. The student hurried on to Castle Bridge, where two small boats were moored. One of them was just about to cast off and quit the plague-ridden city.

"If the Lord spares our lives and the wind serves us, we shall sail to Grönsund, on Falster," the captain said, and he asked the name of this student who wanted to go with them.

"Ludvig Holberg," the student said, and at that time it sounded like any other name. Now it resounds as one of Denmark's proudest names, but he was then only a young student, and unknown.

The boat slipped past the castle, and before daybreak they came to the open sea. A light breeze sprang up and the sails filled. The student sat down with the wind in his face and fell asleep. And that wasn't exactly an advisable thing to do! On the third morning the boat was already at Falster.

"Do you know of anyone in this place with whom I can live cheaply?" Holberg asked the captain.

"I believe you had best go to the ferryman's wife at Borrehouse," he said. "If you want to be polite, call her Mother Sören Sörensen Möller, but she may turn angry if you show her too much politeness. Her husband is under arrest for some crime or other, and she runs the ferry herself. What fists she has!"

The student shouldered his knapsack and went to the ferry house. The door was not locked, so he lifted the latch and entered a brick-floored room in which a large folding bed with a big furred cover was the most noticeable piece of furniture. A white hen, with her chickens around her, was tied to the bedstead. She had upset her drinking dish, and water ran across the floor. No one was there or in the next room, except a little child who lay in a cradle.

The ferryboat came back with only one person on board—whether man or woman was hard to say. This person was wrapped in a great cloak, with a hood that covered the head.

When the boat was docked, it was a woman who entered the room. She had an impressive air as she straightened up and looked at him. Two proud eyes were set under her dark brows. It was Mother Sören, the ferryman's wife, though rooks, crows, and jackdaws could scream out another name by which we would know her better.

Glum she looked, and little enough she cared for talk, but it was settled that the student would stay and board with her for an undetermined time, until things went well again in Copenhagen.

Now and then some honest fellows from the neighboring town dropped in at the ferryhouse. Among them were Frank, the cutler, and Sivert, the customs collector, who came to drink a mug of ale and to chat with the student. He was a thoughtful young man who knew what's what, as they said. He read Latin and Greek, and was well posted in many fields of knowledge.

"The less one knows, the lighter his burden," said Mother Sören.

One day when Holberg watched her wash clothes in strong lye, and chop up knotty stumps for firewood, he told her:

"You work too hard."

"That's my business," she said.

"Have you had to toil and slave this way ever since you were a child?"

"Read the answer in my hands," she said, and showed him her two hands, small but strong and hard, with broken nails. "You know how to read. Read them."

At Christmastime there was a heavy snowfall. The cold made itself at home, and the winds blew as bitterly as if they were dashing acid in people's faces. Mother Sören didn't care. She flung on her cloak, drew up the hood, and went about her business. When the house grew dark early in the afternoon, she would throw pine knots on the fire and sit by it to darn her stockings, for she had no one to do it for her. As evening came on she talked with the student more than she usually did. She spoke of her husband:

"By accident he killed a captain from Dragor, and for this they put him in chains and sentenced him to three years of hard labor on the King's Island. He is only an ordinary sailor, so the law must take its course, you know."

"The law applies to the upper classes too," Holberg said.

"Do you believe that?" Mother Sören stared into the fire, and then went on. "Do you know the story of Kay Lykke, who ordered one of his churches torn down? When Mads, the pastor, thundered from the pulpit against this, he had Mads clapped in irons and thrown in prison. Then he appointed himself judge, found Mads guilty, condemned him, and had his head struck off. That was no accident, yet Kay Lykke was never punished."

"He was within his right, according to the custom of his time," Holberg said. "We have come a long way since then."

"Try to make fools believe you." Mother Sören got up and went into the next room where Toesen, her little child, lay in the cradle. When she had tidied and aired the cradle, she made the student's bed. He had the big furred cover, for though he was born in Norway he felt the cold more than she did.

New Year's Day dawned clear and sunny. It was so cold that the snowdrifts were hard enough for one to walk across them. The bells in the village were ringing for church, as student Holberg wrapped himself in his heavy cloak to set off for town. Rooks flew screeching over Börrehouse, and so did the crows and jackdaws. They made such a racket that you could scarcely hear the bells. Mother Sören stood outside, filling a brass kettle with snow, to melt over the fire for drinking water. She gazed up at the dark swarm of birds and thought her own thoughts.

Student Holberg went to church and on his way back he passed the house of Sivert, the customs collector. Sivert invited him in to warm himself from a bowl of mulled ale, sweetened with syrup and ginger. They started to talk about Mother Sören, but the customs collector knew little about her. Indeed, there were few who did. "She is not a native of Falster," he said, "and she has probably seen better days. Her husband is a common sailor, with a violent temper. He killed a captain on

Dragör, and, though he used to beat his wife, she always sticks up for him."

"I would never stand for that," said the customs collector's wife. "I too come of better stock. My father wove stockings for the king."

"So naturally you married one of the king's officers," Holberg said, with a bow to her husband.

Twelfth Night came, and Mother Sören lighted for Holberg a candle of the Three Kings—that is, three small tallow candles—which she herself had prepared.

"A candle for each man!" said Holberg.

"Each man?" she exclaimed, and looked at him hard.

"Each of the wise men from the east," Holberg said.

"Oh, that's how you meant it," she said, and sat in silence for a while. But on that evening of the Three Kings, he learned a great deal about her that he had not known.

"You are fond of the man you are wedded to," Holberg said, "yet people tell me he daily mistreated you."

"That concerns no one but me," Mother Sören declared. "The blows would have done me good had they fallen when I was a child. Now they probably fall for my sins. I only know the good he has done me." She stood up straight. "When I lay ill and weak among the sand dunes, and no one would come near me except perhaps the rooks, the crows, and the jackdaws, who came to pick at me, he carried me in his arms, and got hard words for bringing such a find on board his ship. I do not come of sickly stock, so I recovered. All of us have our faults, and Sören has his. One must not judge the horse by his halter. With him I have led a more pleasant life than I did with him whom they called the highest and most gallant one of all the king's men. I have been married to Governor Gyldenlöve, half brother to the king. Afterward I took Palle Dyre. Good or bad, each has his own way, and I have mine. That was a long story, and now you know it."

Mother Sören went out of the room.

So this was Marie Grubbe, so strangely does the ball of fortune turn. She did not live to see many more feasts of the Three Kings. Holberg wrote that she died in June, 1716, but he did not write, for he did not know, that when Mother Sören, as they called her, lay dead in Borrehouse, a flock of large black birds flew over the roof in silence. They did not scream, and it was as if they knew that at funerals one must be quiet. As soon as she was in her grave, the birds departed, but on that same evening the birds were seen in enormous numbers over her old estate in Jutland. Rooks, crows, and jackdaws, screamed to each other as if they had much to tell. Perhaps they croaked of him who robbed them of their eggs and young ones when he was a boy—the peasant boy who received an iron garter on the King's Island—and also of the highborn young lady who died a ferrywoman at Grönsund.

"Bra! Bra!" they croaked. And "Bra, Bra!" the whole tribe croaked when the old castle was torn down. "And this they cry still, though there is nothing left to croak about," said the parish clerk, when he told the story. "The family died out, the castle was torn down, and where it stood the new hen house now stands, with its gilded weathercock on the roof and Chicken Grethe inside. There she sits, well satisfied with her cosy residence, for if she had not come here she would have gone to the workhouse!" The pigeons cooed above her, the turkeys clucked, and the ducks quacked around her. "No one knew her," they said. "She had no relatives. By an act of charity she came here, and children she had none!"

Nevertheless, she had ancestors, though she did not know of them, nor did the parish clerk, for all the manuscripts he had in his table drawer. But one of the old crows knew, and he told about it. From its mother and its grandmother, it had heard tell of Chicken Grethe's mother and grandmother, whom we know too. We know how, as a child, she rode over the drawbridge and looked about proudly, as if the whole world and all the bird nests in it belonged to her. We also saw her on the sand dunes, and last at the ferryhouse. Her granddaughter, last of her line, had come home again where the old castle had stood and where the wild birds croaked. But she sat among her tame fowls, known by them and on friendly terms with them.

Chicken Grethe had nothing more to wish for. She was happy to die and old enough to die.

"Grave, grave!" the crows croaked.

And Chicken Grethe was buried in a good grave. No one knows where it lies except the old crow, if he isn't dead too.

Now we know the story of the old castle, and of all Chicken Grethe's family.

THE COMET (1869)

Now there came a comet with its shiny nucleus and its menacing tail. People from the great castles and people from the poor huts gazed at it. So did the crowd in the street, and so did the man who went his solitary way across the pathless heath. Everyone had his own thoughts. "Come and look at the omen from heaven. Come out and see this marvelous sight," they cried, and everyone hastened to look.

But a little boy and his mother still stayed inside their room. The tallow candle was burning and the mother thought she saw a bit of wood shaving in the light. The tallow formed a jagged edge around the candle, and then it curled. The mother believed these were signs that her son would soon die. The wood shaving was circling toward him. This was an old superstition, but she believed it. The little boy lived many more years on earth. Indeed he lived to see the comet return sixty years later.

The boy did not see the wood shaving in the candlelight, and his thoughts were not about the comet which then, for the first time in his life, shone brightly in the sky. He sat quietly with an earthenware bowl before him. The bowl was filled with soapy water, into which he dipped the head of a clay pipe. Then he put the pipe stem in his mouth, and blew soap bubbles, large and small. They quivered and spun in beautiful colors. They changed from yellow to red, and from red to purple or blue and then they turned bright green, like leaves when the sun shines through them.

The boy's mother said, "May God grant you many more years on Earth—as many years as the bubbles you are blowing."

"So many, so many!" he cried. "I can never blow all the soapy water into bubbles. There goes one year, there goes another one; see how they fly!" he exclaimed, as bubbles came loose from his pipe and floated away. A few of them blew into his eye, where they burned and smarted, and made his tears flow. In every bubble he saw a picture of the future, glimmering and glistening.

"This is the time to look at the comet," cried their neighbors. "Come outdoors. Don't sit in your room."

The mother took her boy by the hand. He had to put aside his clay pipe and stop playing with the soap bubbles, because there was a comet to see.

The boy saw the bright ball of fire, with its shining tail. Some said it was three yards long, while others insisted it was several million yards long—such a difference.

Most of the people who said these things were dead and buried when the comet came again. But the little boy, toward whom the wood shaving had circled and of whom his mother thought, "He will soon die," still lived on, though he had grown old and his hair was white. "White hairs are the flowers of age," the saying goes, and he had many such flowers. He was an old schoolmaster. The school children thought him very wise and learned, because he knew history, and geography, and all there is to be known about the heavens and the stars.

"Everything comes again," he said. "If you will pay attention to people and events, you will learn that they always come back. There may be a hundred years between, or many hundreds of years, but once again we shall see the same character, in another coat and in another country." And the schoolmaster then told them about William Tell, who was forced to shoot an apple from his son's head, but before he shot the arrow he hid another one in his shirt, to shoot into the heart of the wicked Gessler. This happened in Switzerland. But many years before, the same thing happened in Denmark to Palnatoke. He too was forced to shoot an apple from his son's head, and he too hid an arrow in his shirt to avenge the cruelty. And more than a thousand years before that, the same story was written in Egypt. It happened before and will happen again, just as sure as the comet returns. "Off it flies into space, and is gone for years, but still it comes back." He spoke of the comet that was expected, the same comet he had seen as a boy.

The schoolmaster knew what went on in the skies, and he thought much about it too, but he did not neglect history and geography. His garden was laid out in the shape of a map of Denmark. In it grew herbs and flowers which flourished in different parts of the land.

"Fetch me peas," he said, and they went to the garden bed that represented Laaland. "Fetch me buckwheat," he said, and they fetched it from Langeland. Lovely blue gentian was planted in Skagen, and the shining Christthorn in Silkeborg. Towns and cities were marked with small statues. Here was the dragon and St. Knud, who stood for Odense. Absalon with the bishop's staff stood for Sorö. The little boat with oars marked the site of Aarhus. In the schoolmaster's garden you could learn the geography of Denmark, but first you had to be instructed by him and that was a pleasure.

Now that the comet was expected again, he told about it,

and he told what people had said in the old days when it last was seen. They had said that a comet year was a good year for wine, and that water could be mixed with this wine without being detected. Therefore the wine merchants thought well of a comet year.

For fourteen days and fourteen nights the sky was clouded over. They could not see the comet, and yet it was there. The old schoolmaster sat in his little chamber next to the schoolroom. The old Bornholm clock of his grandfather's time stood in the corner, though its heavy lead weights moved neither up nor down, nor did its pendulum ever swing. The little cuckoo that used to come out to call the passing hours had long ago stopped doing his duty. The clock neither struck nor ticked. The clock was decidedly out of order.

But the old clavichord at which he sat had been made in his parents' time, and it still had a tune or two left in it. The strings could still play. Tremulous though they were, they could play for him the melodies of a whole lifetime. As the old man heard them, he remembered many things, both pleasant and sad, that had happened in the long years which had gone by since he was a little boy and saw the comet. Now that the comet had come again, he remembered what his mother had said about the wood shaving circling toward him. He remembered the fine soap bubbles he had blown, one for every year of his life he had said as he looked at them glistening and gleaming in wonderful colors. He saw in them all his pleasures and sorrow—everything, both the good and the bad. He saw the child at his play and the youth with his fancies. His whole life, iridescent and bright, floated before his eyes. And in that splendor he saw his future too, in bubbles of time to come.

First, the old man heard from the strings of the clavichord the melodies of times past, and saw the bubbles of years gone by, colored with memories. He heard his grandmother's knitting song:

Surely no Amazon
The first stockings knit.

And then the strings played the songs his old nurse used to sing for him:

There were so many dangers
In this world to pass through
For people who were young
And only little knew.

Now the melodies of his first ball were playing, for the minuet and molinasky—soft melancholy tunes that brought tears to the old man's eyes. A roaring war march, then a psalm, then happy tunes. The years whirled past as if they were those bubbles he blew when he was a little boy.

His eyes were turned toward the window. A cloud billowed across the sky, and as it passed he saw the comet with its shining nucleus and its shining, misty veil. It seemed to him as though it were only yesterday evening when he had last seen that comet, yet a whole busy lifetime lay between that evening and this. Then he was a child, looking through bubbles into the future; now those bright bubbles were all behind him. Once more he had a child's outlook and a child's faith. His eyes sparkled, and his hands struck the keys. There was the sound of a breaking string.

"Come out and see," cried his neighbors. "The comet is here, and the sky is clear. Come out and look!"

The old schoolmaster did not answer. He had gone where he

could see more clearly. His soul was on a journey far greater than the comet's, and the realm to which it went was far more spacious than that in which the comet moved.

Again the comet was seen from the high castle and from the lowly hut. The crowd in the street gazed up at it, and so did the man who went his solitary way across the pathless heath. But the schoolmaster's soul was seen by God, and by those dear ones who had gone before him, and whom he longed to see.

THE CANDLES (1870)

There was once a big wax candle who had the highest opinion of his merits. "I," he said, "am made of the purest wax, cast in the best mold. I burn more brilliantly than any other candle, and I outlast them all. I belong in the high chandelier or the silver candlestick."

"What a delightful life you must lead," the tallow candle admitted. "I am only tallow. Just a tallow dip. But it's a comfort to think how much better off I am than the taper. He's only dipped twice, while I am dipped eight times to make a thick and respectable candle of me. I'm satisfied. To be sure it would be better to be born of wax than of tallow, and a lucky thing to be shaped in a mold, but one isn't asked how he wants to be born. Your place is in the big rooms with glass chandeliers. Mine is in the kitchen. But the kitchen is a good place too. All the food in the house comes from there."

"There are more important things in the world than food," the wax candle boasted. "There's the glitter of good society in which I shine. Why, I and all my family are invited to a ball that's being given here this very evening."

No sooner had he said this than all the wax candles were sent for. But the tallow candle was not left behind. The mistress of the house took it in her own hand and carried it to the kitchen, where a poor boy waited with his basket full of potatoes and a few apples that she had given him.

"And here's a candle for you too, my little friend," she told him. "Your mother can use it to work by when she sits up late at night."

The lady's small daughter stood close beside her mother, and when she heard the magic words "late at night," she forgot to be shy. "I'm going to stay up late tonight too!" she exclaimed. "We are to have a ball this evening, and I'm to wear my big red ribbon." No candle ever could shine like the eyes of a child.

"Happiness is a blessed thing to see," the tallow candle thought to himself. "I mustn't forget how it looks, for I certainly shan't see it again." They put him in the basket and closed the lid. Away the boy went with it.

"Where can he be taking me?" the candle wondered. "I may have to live with poor people who don't even own a brass candlestick, while the wax candle sits in silver and beams at all the best people. How fine it must be to shine in good company. But this is what I get for being tallow, not wax."

And the candle did come to live with poor people. They were a widow and her three children, who had a low-ceilinged room across the way from the well-to-do house.

"God bless our neighbor for all that she gave us," the widow said. "This good candle will burn far into the night."

She struck a match to it.

"Fut, fie," he sputtered. "What a vile smelling match she lights me with. Would anyone offer such a kitchen match to the wax candle in the well-to-do house across the way?"

There the candles were lighted too. They made the street bright as carriages came rumbling with guests dressed in their best for the ball. The music struck up.

"Now the ball's beginning." The tallow candle burned

brighter as he remembered the happy little girl whose face was more shining than the light of all those wax candles. "I'll never see anything like that again."

The smallest of the poor children reached up, for she was very small, and put her arms around the necks of her brother and sister. What she had to tell them was so important that it had to be whispered. "Tonight we're going to have—just think of it—warm potatoes, this very night."

Her face beamed with happiness and the candle beamed right back at her. He saw happiness again, and a gladness as great as when the little girl in the well-to-do house said, "We're having a ball this evening, and I'm to wear my red ribbon."

"Is it such a treat to get warm potatoes?" the candle wondered. "Little children must manage to be happy here, too." He wept tallow tears of joy, and more than that a candle cannot do.

The table was spread and the potatoes were eaten. How good they tasted! It was a real feast. There was an apple for everyone, and the smallest child said grace:

Now thanks, dear Lord, I give to Thee
That Thou again hast filled me. Amen.

"And didn't I say it nicely?" the little girl asked.

"Don't say such things," her mother told her. "Just thank the good Lord for filling you up."

The children went to bed, were kissed good night, and fell fast asleep. Their mother sat up late and sewed to make a living for them and for herself. From the well-to-do house came light and music. But the stars overhead shone on all the houses, rich or poor, with the same light, clear and kind.

"This has been a wonderful evening," the tallow candle told

himself. "Can the wax candle have had any better time of it in his silver candlestick? I'd like to know that before I'm burned out."

He remembered the two happy children, one face lighted up by the wax candle, the other shining in the tallow candle's light. One was happy as the other. Yes, that is the whole story!

THE MOST INCREDIBLE THING (1870)

Whosoever could do the most incredible thing was to have the king's daughter and half of his kingdom.

The young men, yes, and the old ones too, bent their heads, their muscles, and their hearts upon winning. To do what they thought was the most incredible thing, two ate themselves to death, and one died of overdrinking. Even the boys in the street practiced spitting on their own backs, which they supposed was the most incredible thing anyone could do.

On a certain day there was to be an exhibition of things most incredible and everyone showed his best work. Judges were appointed, ranging from children of three to old men of ninety. It was a grand exposition of things out of the ordinary, but everybody promptly agreed that most incredible of all was a great hall clock—an extraordinary contraption, outside and in.

When the clock struck, out came lifelike figures to tell the hour. There were twelve separate performances of these moving figures, with speaking and singing. People said that nothing so incredible had ever before been seen.

The clock struck one, and there stood Moses on the mountain, writing in the tablets of the law the first great commandment: "There is only one true God." The clock struck two, and there were Adam and Eve, just as they first met in the Garden of Eden. Were ever two people so lucky! They didn't own so much as a clothes closet, and they didn't need one.

At the stroke of three, the three Holy Kings appeared. One was as black as a coal, but he couldn't help that. The sun had blackened him. These kings brought incense and precious gifts. When the stroke of four sounded, the seasons advanced in their order. Spring carried a budding bough of beech, on which a cuckoo sang. Summer had for her sign a grasshopper on a ripening ear of wheat. Autumn had only an empty stork's nest, for the birds had flown away. Winter's tame crow perched on the corner of the stove, and told old tales of bygone days. At five o'clock there was a procession of the five senses. Sight was represented by a man who made spectacles. Hearing was a noisy coppersmith. Smell was a flower girl with violets for sale. Taste came dressed as a cook. Feeling was a mourner with crepe down to his heels. As the clock struck six, there sat a gambler, throwing dice for the highest cast of all, and they fell with the sixes up. Then came the seven days of the week, or they might be the seven deadly sins. People could not be sure which they were, for they were not easy to distinguish. Next came a choir of monks to sing the eight o'clock evensong. At the stroke of nine, the nine muses appeared. One was an astronomer, one kept the books of history, and the others were connected with the theater. Ten o'clock struck, and Moses came forth again, this time with the tables on which were written all ten of God's commandments. When the clock struck again, boys and girls danced out. They played and sang this song:

All the way to Heaven
The clock struck eleven.

And eleven it struck. Then came the stroke of twelve. Out marched the night watchman, wearing his cap and carrying his morning star, which is a truncheon tipped with spikes. He sang the old watch song:

'Twas at the midnight hour

Our Savior He was born—and as he sang, the roses about him unfolded into the heads of angels with rainbow-tinted wings.

It was good to hear. It was charming to see. The whole thing was a work of extraordinary craftsmanship, and everyone agreed that it was the most incredible thing. The artist who had made it was young, generous, and sincere, a true friend, and a great help to his poor father and mother. He was altogether worthy of the princess and of half the kingdom.

On the day that they were to proclaim who had won, the whole town was bedecked and be-draped. The princess sat on her throne. It had been newly stuffed with horsehair for the occasion, but it was still far from comfortable or pleasant. The judges winked knowingly at the man they had chosen, who stood there so happy and proud. His fortune was made, for had he not done the most incredible thing!

"No!" a tall, bony, powerful fellow bawled out. "Leave it to me; I am the man to do the most incredible thing," and then he swung his ax at the craftsman's clock. Crack, crash, smash! There lay the whole thing. Here rolled the wheels, and there flew the hairsprings. It was wrecked and ruined. "I did that," said the lout. "My work beat his, and bowled you over, all in one stroke. I have done the most incredible thing."

"To destroy such a work of art!" said the judges. "Why, it's the most incredible thing we've ever seen." And the people said so, too. So he was awarded the princess and half the kingdom, because a law is a law, even if it happens to be a most incredible one.

They blew trumpets from the ramparts and the city towers, and they announced, "The wedding will now take place." The princess was not especially happy about it, but she looked pretty and she wore her most expensive clothes. The church was at its best by candlelight, late in the evening. The ladies of the court sang in processions, and escorted the bride. The lords sang and accompanied the groom. From the way he strutted and swaggered along, you'd think that nothing could ever bowl him over.

Then the singing stopped. It was so still that you could have heard a pin fall in the street. But it was not quiet for long. Crash! crash! the great church doors flew open, and boom! boom! all the works of the clock came marching down the church aisle and halted between the bride and the groom.

Dead men cannot walk the earth. That's true, but a work of art does not die. Its shape may be shattered, but the spirit of art cannot be broken. The spirit of art jested, and that was no joke.

To all appearances it stood there as if it were whole and had never been wrecked. The clock struck one hour right after another, from one to twelve, and all the figures poured forth. First Moses came, shining as if bright flames issued from his forehead. He cast the heavy stone tablets of the law at the bridegroom's feet and tied them to the church floor. "I cannot lift them again," said Moses, "for you have broken my arms. Stand where you are!"

Then came Adam and Eve, the three Wise Men of the East, and the four Seasons. Each told him the disagreeable truth. "Shame on you!" But he was not ashamed.

All the figures of all the hours marched out of the clock, and they grew wondrous big. There was scarcely room for the living people. And at the stroke of twelve, out strode the watchman, with his cap and his many-spiked morning star. There was a strange commotion. The watchman went straight to the bridegroom, and smote him on the forehead with his morning star.

"Lie where you are," said the watchman. "A blow for a blow. We have taken out vengeance and the master's too, so now we will vanish."

And vanish they did, every cogwheel and figure. But the candles of the church flared up like flowers of fire, and the gilded stars under the roof cast down long clear shafts of light, and the organ sounded though no man had touched it. The people all said that they had lived to see the most incredible thing.

"Now," the princess commanded, "summon the right man, the craftsman who made the work of art. He shall be my husband and my lord."

He stood beside her in the church. All the people were in his train. Everyone was happy for him, everyone blessed him, and there was no one who was envious. And that was the most incredible thing.

DANISH POPULAR LEGENDS (1870)

Denmark is rich in old legends of heroes, of churches and manor houses, of hills and fields, and of the bottomless moorland. These stories date from the days of the great plague, from times of war, and from times of peace. They live on in books or on the tongues of people. They fly far about like a flock of birds, but they are as different, one from another, as the thrush is from the owl, and the wood pigeon from the gull. Listen to me, and I will tell you some of these legends.

I

In the olden days, when invaders were ravaging the Danish countryside, it happened that a pitched battle was fought, and the Danes won. That evening, many dead and many wounded men lay on the stricken field. One of these was an enemy, who had lost both his legs by a shot. Nearby a Danish soldier had just taken a flask filled with beer from his pocket and was about to put it to his mouth when the desperately wounded man begged him for a drink. As the soldier bent down to give the bottle to his enemy, the wounded man discharged his pistol at him, but he missed his aim. The soldier took his bottle back and drank half of it. As he handed the rest to his enemy, his only comment was, "You rascal, now you will get only half of it."

When the king was told of this, in memory of the deed he granted to the soldier and to his descendants a noble coat of arms on which was blazoned a bottle, half full.

II

There is a beautiful tradition worth telling of the church bell at Farum. Here the parsonage and the church stand side by side. It was a dark night, late in the fall. The minister was sitting at work upon his Sunday sermon when he heard the large church bell sound, very lightly and very strangely. No wind was blowing, and he could not account for the noise.

The minister took his keys and went to the church. As he entered it, the bell tone ceased, but he heard a faint sigh from the belfry.

"Who is there?" he asked in a loud voice. "Who is disturbing the peace of this church?" Footsteps pattered down the bell tower steps, and he saw a little boy coming toward him.

"Don't be angry," the boy said. "I slipped in here when the bell was rung for vespers. My mother is very ill—" Tears choked him, and he could not speak. The minister patted him on the cheek and encouraged the boy to tell his story frankly.

"They say that my mother—my sweet and good mother—is going to die. But I've heard tell that, when people are sick unto death, they may live to be well again if someone dares enter the church and at midnight scrape a little rust from the great church bell. That will keep death away, so I came here and hid myself till I heard the clock strike twelve. I was afraid. I thought of the dead people rising from their graves, and of their coming into the church, and I dared not look out in the churchyard. But I said the Lord's Prayer, and scraped the rust off of the bell."

"Come, my brave child," said the minister. "The good Lord

will not forsake you or your mother." They went together to the poor cottage where the sick woman lay. She was in a sound and peaceful sleep.

God granted that she should live, and His blessings shone on her and her child.

III

This is a legend they tell about a poor young fellow, Paul Vendelbo, who came to be a great man, highly honored. He was born in Jutland. After he had struggled hard and studied so well that he got through his examination as a scholar, he felt a still greater ambition to be a soldier and to stroll about in faraway lands.

One day he was walking along the ramparts of Copenhagen with two young prosperous comrades. As he was telling them of his ambition, all of a sudden, he stopped and looked up at the window of a house where the young daughter of a professor was sitting. They all found her astonishingly pretty. When Paul's comrades saw how he blushed, they said as a joke:

"Paul, if you can get her to give you a kiss in front of the window where we can see it, we will give the money you need to travel. Then you can see if fortune favors you better abroad than at home."

Paul Vendelbo went into the house and knocked at the parlor door. "My father is not at home," the young girl told him.

"Don't be angry," he begged her, as the blood rushed up into his cheeks, "but it's not your father I want." Then he told her frankly of his wholehearted ambition to adventure out into the world and make an honorable name for himself. He told her of his two friends who were standing outside and how they had promised him his traveling expenses if, of her own free will, she would kiss him at the open window. He looked at her so bashfully, so honorably, and so frankly, that her anger died away.

"It is wrong for you to propose such a thing to a modest young girl," she told him. "But you look so honest that I won't stand in the way of your good fortune." She led him to the window and gave him a kiss.

His comrades kept their bargain and gave him the money. He went into the service of the Tsar of Russia, made a name for himself in the battle of Pultawa, and honors were heaped upon him. Afterward, when Denmark stood in need of him, he came home to become a man of might in the army and in the council of the king. Lövenörn, they called him, which means Lion-Eagle.

One day he again entered the professor's modest room. Again, it was not the professor he wanted, but the professor's daughter, Ingeborg Vinding—the girl who gave him the kiss with which his good fortune began. Fourteen days later Paul Vendelbo Lövenörn celebrated his wedding.

IV

The enemy once made a great attack on the Danish island of Fyen. Only one village was left standing, and this was soon to be sacked and burned.

Two poor people lived in a low-roofed house at the edge of the town. It was a dark winter's night, and the enemy were expected at any minute. The two poor, anxious people opened their psalm book to see if they could find anything in it to help or to comfort them. They opened their book and turned to the psalm, "A Mighty Fortress Is Our God."

Full of confidence, they sang the psalm, and their faith was renewed. They went to bed and slept well in the care of the Lord. In the morning, when they awoke, they found the room entirely dark. There was no glimmer of daylight, and the door would not open when they tried it. Then they climbed to the loft and opened a trapdoor in the roof, from which they saw that it was broad daylight. But a heavy snow had fallen in the night. It had drifted over their whole house and hidden it from the enemies who had pillaged and burned the town during the night. The two people clasped their hands in thankfulness, and again they sang, "A Mighty Fortress Is Our God," for he had shielded them and raised a rampart of snow around their home.

V

In North Seeland they tell of a dark mystery that challenges one's imagination. The church of Roervig lies far out among the sand dunes by the stormy Kattegat. One evening a great ship came to anchor off the shore. It seemed to be a Russian man-of-war. That night there was a knock at the parsonage door, and several people, armed and masked, demanded that the minister put on his robes and come with them, out to the church. They promised to pay him well, and they threatened him if he should refuse to go. He went.

He found the church lighted. Unknown people were gathered there, and all was in deep silence. A bride and groom waited in front of the altar. The magnificent clothes they wore suggested the highest rank, but the bride was deathly pale. When the marriage ceremony ended, a shot rang out, and the bride fell dead at the altar. The people took her corpse and went away with it. Next morning, the ship was gone, and to this day no one has been able to give any explanation of these happenings.

The minister who took part in it wrote the whole story down in his Bible, which his family has kept to this day. The old church still stands between the sand dunes, near the tossing waters of the Kattegat, and the story still lives in memory and in writing.

VI

I must tell you one more church legend. On the island of Falster, which is part of Denmark, there lived a lady of rank and wealth. She had no children, and her family was about to die out. So she took a part of her wealth and built a magnificent church. When it was finished and the candles were lighted, she knelt at the altar and prayed that, for her pious gift, God would grant her life upon this Earth as long as her church should stand.

The years went by. Her relatives died. Her old friends, her acquaintances, and all her old servants were laid in their graves. But she, who had made such an evil wish, did not die. Generation after generation grew up and were strangers to her. She did not go to see anyone, and no one came to see her. She wasted away in a long dotage, abandoned and alone. Her senses grew dull, and she was like someone asleep, but not like a dead person. Every Christmas Eve life flashed up in her for a moment, and she got back the use of her voice. Then she would order her new servants to put her in an oak coffin, and carry it to the graveyard by the church. The minister was asked to come and receive her commands. They laid her in the coffin, and brought it to the church. As she wished, every Christmas night the minister came through the choir up to the coffin and raised the coffin lid for the weary old lady who lay there without finding rest.

"Is my church still standing?" she would ask in a tremulous voice, and when the minister answered, "It still stands," she would give a deep sigh and sadly fall back in her coffin. The minister closed down the lid and came again on next Christmas Eve, and the next, and again and again.

Now there is no stone of the church left standing, no trace of the buried dead. A large whitethorn grows in the field there, and it blooms every spring as a sign of the resurrection of life. It is said that it grows on the spot where they placed the coffin of the highborn lady, and where her dust at last became dust of this earth.

VII

There is an old saying that when our Lord drove the rebellious angels out of heaven, He let some of them fall among the hills, where they still live and are called hobgoblins, or trolls. They always flee in terror when they hear thunder, which they believe is the wrath of Heaven. Others fell down in the alder marshes. These are called elves, and among them the women are very handsome to look at, but they are not to be trusted. Their backs are as hollow as a baker's dough trough. Others fell down in old farms and houses. These became dwarfs and goblins. Sometimes they have dealings with men, and many strange stories are told about them.

In Jutland, a hobgoblin lived with many other trolls in a large hill. One of his daughters was married to the village blacksmith, who was a bad man. He beat his wife until at last she tired of it. Just as he was about to beat her one day, she took a horseshoe and broke it upon him. She had such tremendous strength that she could easily have broken him in pieces too. He thought about this, and did not beat her again, but gossip spread the story abroad, and the country people no longer respected her. Now that they knew her to be the troll's daughter, no one in the parish would have anything to do with her. And the hobgoblin heard of this. One Sunday, the blacksmith, his wife, and other parishioners were in the churchyard, waiting for the parson. The blacksmith's wife looked out over the bay, where fog was rising.

"Here comes father," she said, "and he is angry." He came, and angry he was. "Will you throw them to me, or would you rather do the catching?" he asked, and looked with greedy eyes upon the church people.

"I'll do the catching," she said, for she knew very well that he would not handle them gently if they fell in his hands. The hobgoblin seized one after another, and flung them over the roof of the church, while his daughter stood on the far side and caught them as gently as she could. From that time on, she got along very nicely with the parishioners. They were afraid of the hobgoblin and his many fellow trolls, who were scattered about the country. The best people could do was to avoid quarreling with him and try to turn his acquaintance to their profit. Everyone knew that trolls had big kettles full of gold, and it was well worthwhile to get a handful of this money. But to do so they had to be as clever and tricky as the farmer of whom I shall tell you. I shall tell you also of the farmer's boy, who tended pigs and was even cleverer than his master.

The farmer had a hill among his fields, which he did not want to leave idle. So he plowed it, but the hobgoblin who lived under the hill came out and asked him:

"How dare you plow my roof?"

"I didn't know it was your roof," the farmer said, "but it is neither to your advantage nor to mine for us to allow the land to lie idle. Let me plow and plant. The first year you may take what is growing above the ground, and I shall reap what grows in the earth. The next year we will change around." The bargain was made, and the first year the farmer planted carrots. The second year he sowed wheat. The hobgoblin got the tops of the carrots and the roots of the wheat. In this way they lived in harmony.

But it happened that there was to be a christening at the farmer's house. He was greatly embarrassed, because he could not very well avoid inviting a hobgoblin with whom he was on such good terms. But if the troll should accept his invitation, the farmer would get a bad name with the minister and with all the other people in the parish. Clever though the farmer usually was this time he didn't know what to do. He mentioned his troubles to the boy who tended his pigs and who was even more clever than he.

"I will help you," the boy said. He took a large bag and went out to the hill where the hobgoblin lived. He knocked and was let in. Then he said that he came to invite the hobgoblin to the christening. The hobgoblin accepted the invitation and promised to come.

"I suppose I'll have to give a christening present, won't I?"

"They usually do," said the boy, and opened his bag. The troll poured money into it.

"Is that enough?"

The boy lifted the bag, and said, "Most people give as much." When all the gold in the big money kettle had been poured into the bag, the boy said, "Nobody gives more—most less."

"Tell me now," said the hobgoblin, "what honored guests are you expecting?"

"Three parsons and a bishop," said the boy. "That's fine. Such gentlemen care only for eating and drinking. They won't bother me. Who else will come?"

"Mother Mary is expected."

"Hm, hm! But I think there will still be a little place for me behind the stove. And who else will be there?"

"Well, there's the Lord."

"Hm! Hm! Hm! You don't say so! But such extremely distinguished guests usually come late and leave early. While they are there I'll just step out for a moment. What sort of music will you have?"

"Drum music," said the boy. "The Lord has ordered a heavy thunder of drum music, to which we shall dance. Drum music it will be."

"Oh, isn't that dreadful!" the hobgoblin cried. "Thank your master for his invitation, but I prefer to stay at home. Doesn't he know that thundering and drumming terrify me and all of my people? Once, when I went for a walk in my younger days, the thunder began drumming, and one of the drumsticks thumped my thigh so hard that the bone cracked. I'll have no more of that sort of music, so just give the farmer my thanks and my present."

The boy took the bag on his back and brought his master a

fortune along with the troll's best wishes.

We have many such legends, but those we have told here ought to be enough for today!

WHAT THE WHOLE FAMILY SAID (1870)

What did the whole family say? Well, listen first to what little Marie said.

It was little Marie's birthday, the most wonderful of all days, she imagined. All her little boy friends and girl friends came to play with her, and she wore her prettiest dress, the one Grandmother, who was now with God, had sewn for her before she went up into the bright, beautiful Heaven. The table in little Marie's room was loaded with presents; there was the prettiest little kitchen, with everything that belongs to a kitchen, and a doll that could close its eyes and say "Ouch!" when you pinched its stomach; yes, and there was also a picture book, with the most wonderful stories, to be read when one could read! But to have many birthdays was more wonderful than all the stories in the book.

"Yes, it's wonderful to be alive," said little Marie. And her godfather added that it was the most beautiful of all fairy tales.

In the next room were both her brothers; they were big boys, one of them nine years old, the other eleven. They thought it was wonderful to be alive, too; that is, to live in their own way, not to be a baby like Marie, but to be real smart schoolboys, to get As on their report cards, to have friendly fights with their comrades, to go skating in the winter and bicycling in the summer, to read about the days of knighthood, with its castles, its drawbridges, and its dungeons, and to hear about new discoveries in Central Africa. On the latter subject, however, one of the boys felt very sad in that he feared everything might be discovered before he grew up, and then there would be no adventure left for him. But Godfather said, "Life itself is the most wonderful adventure, and you have a part in it yourself."

These children lived on the first floor of the house; in the flat above them lived another branch of the family, also with children, but these all had long since been shaken from their mother's apron strings, so big were they; one son was seventeen, and another twenty, but the third one was very old, said little Marie; he was twenty-five, and engaged to be married. They were all very well off, had nice parents, good clothes, and were well educated, and they knew what they wanted. "Look forward," they said. "Away with all the old fences! Let's have an open view into the wide world! That's the greatest thing we know of! Godfather is right—life is the most wonderful fairy tale!"

Father and Mother, both older people—naturally, they would have to be older than the children—said, with smiling lips and smiling eyes and hearts, "How young these young people are! Things usually don't happen in this world just as they expect them to, yet life goes on. Life is a strange and wonderful adventure."

On the next floor—a little closer to Heaven, as we say when people live in an attic—lived Godfather. He was old, and yet so young in mind, always in a good humor, and he certainly could tell stories, many and long ones. He had traveled the world over, and his room was filled with pretty tokens from every country. Pictures were hung from ceiling to floor, and some of the windowpanes were of red or yellow glass; if one looked through them, the whole world lay in sunshine, however gray the weather might be outside. Green plants grew in a large glass case, and in an enclosure therein swam goldfish; they looked at one as if they knew many things they didn't care to talk about. There was always a sweet fragrance of flowers, even in the wintertime. And then a great fire blazed in the fireplace; it was such a pleasure to sit and look into it and hear how it crackled and spat.

"It refreshes old memories to me," said Godfather. And to little Marie there seemed to appear many pictures in the fire.

But in the big bookcase close by stood real books; one of these Godfather often read, and this he called the Book of Books; it was the Bible. In it was pictured the history of the world and the history of all mankind, of the creation, the flood, the kings, and the King of Kings.

"All that has happened and all that will happen is written in this book," said Godfather; "so infinitely much in one single book! Just think of it! Yes, everything that a human being has to pray for is entered there, and said in a few words in the prayer 'Our Father'! It is the drop of mercy! It is the pearl of comfort from God. It is laid as a gift on the baby's cradle, laid on the child's heart. Little child, keep it safely; don't ever lose it, however big you may grow, and you will never be left alone on life's changeful way; it will shine within you and you will never be lost!"

Godfather's eyes radiated joy. Once, in his youth, they had wept, "and this was also good," he said. "That was a time of trial, when everything looked dark and gray. Now I have sunshine within me and around me. The older one grows, the clearer one sees, in both prosperity and misfortune, that our

Lord always is with us and that life is the most beautiful of all fairy tales, and this he alone can give us—and so it will be into eternity."

"Yes, it is wonderful to be alive!" said little Marie.

So said also the small and the big boys, as well as Father and Mother and the whole family—but first of all, Godfather, who had had so much experience and was the oldest of them all. He knew all stories, all the fairy tales. And it was right from the bottom of his heart that he said, "Life is the most wonderful fairy tale of all!"

GREAT-GRANDFATHER (1870)

Great-grandfather was so lovable, wise and good. All of us looked up to Great-grandfather. As far back as I can remember, he was really called "Father's Father," and "Mother's Father" as well, but when my Brother Frederick's little son came along he was promoted, and got the title of "Great-grandfather." He could not expect to go any higher than that.

He was very fond of us all, but he did not appear to be fond of our times. "Old times were the good times," he used to say. "Quiet and genuine they were. In these days there's too much hurrying and turning everything upside down. The young folk lay down the law, and even speak about the kings as if they are their equals. Any ne'er-do-well can sop a rag in dirty water and wring it out over the head of an honorable man."

Great-grandfather would get angry and red in the face when he talked of such things, but soon he would smile his kindly, sympathetic smile, and say, "Oh, well! I may be a bit wrong. I belong to the old days, and I can't quite get a foothold in the new. May God guide us and show us the right way to go."

When Great-grandfather got started on the old days, it seemed to me as if they came back. I would imagine myself riding along in a gilded coach, with footmen in fine livery. I saw the guilds move their signs and march in procession with their banners aloft, preceded by music. And I attended the merry Christmas festivities, where people in fancy dress played games of forfeit.

True enough, in the old days dreadfully cruel and horrible things used to be done. There was torture, rack and wheel, and bloodshed, but even these horrible things had an excitement about them that fascinated me. But I also thought of many pleasant things. I used to imagine how things were when the Danish nobility freed the peasants, and when the Danish Crown Prince abolished slave trading. It was marvelous to hear Great-grandfather talk of all these things, and to hear him tell of the days of his youth. But I think the times even earlier than that were the very best times of all—so mighty and glorious.

"They were barbarous times," Brother Frederick said. "Thank heaven we are well rid of them." He used to say this right out to Great-grandfather. This was most improper, I know, but just the same I always had great respect for Frederick. He was my oldest brother, and he used to say he was old enough to be my father—but then he was always saying the oddest things. He had graduated with the highest honors, and was so quick and clever in his work at Father's office that Father meant to make him a partner before long. Of us all, he was the one with whom Great-grandfather talked most, but they always began to argue, for they did not get along well together. They did not understand each other, those two, and the family said they never would, but even as young as I was, I soon felt that they were indispensable to each other. Great-grandfather would listen with the brightest look in his eyes while Frederick spoke of or read aloud about scientific progress, and new discoveries in the laws of nature, and about all the other marvels of our times.

"The human race gets cleverer, but it doesn't get better," Great-grandfather would say. "People invent the most terrible and harmful weapons with which to kill and injure each other."

"Then the war will be over that much sooner," Frederick would tell him. "No need now for us to wait seven years for the blessings of peace. The world is full-blooded, and it needs to be bled now and then. That is a necessity."

One day Frederick told him of something that actually happened in a small country and in our own times. The mayor's clock—the large one on the town hall—kept time for the whole town and for everyone who lived there. The clock did not run very well, but that didn't matter nor did it keep anyone from looking to it for the time. But by and by railroads were built in that country, and in all countries railroads run by the clock. One must therefore be sure of the time and know it exactly, or there will be collisions. At the railroad station they had a clock that was absolutely reliable, and exactly in accord with the sun. But as the mayor's was not, everyone went by the railroad clock.

I laughed, and thought the story a funny one, but Great-grandfather did not laugh. He became very serious.

"There is a profound meaning in what you have told me," he declared, "and I understood the thought that prompted you to tell me the story. There's a moral in the clockwork. It reminds me of another clock—my parents' simple, old-fashioned Bornholm clock, with lead weights. It measured out the time of their lives and of my childhood. Perhaps it didn't run any too well, but it ran just the same. We would look at the hour hand and believe in it, with never a thought about the works inside. In those days the machinery of government was like that old clock. Everybody believed in it and only looked at the hour hand. Now government machinery is like a clock in a glass case, so that one can look directly into the works and see the wheels turning and whizzing around. Sometimes we become quite frightened over this spring or that wheel, and then I wonder how it is possible for all these complicated parts to tell the right time. I have lost my childish belief in the rightness of the old clock. That is the weakness of this age."

Great-grandfather would talk on until he became quite angry. He and Frederick could not agree, yet they could not bear to be separated—"just like old times and new." Both of them felt this—and so did our whole family—when Frederick was to set out on his journey to faraway America. It was on business for the company, so the journey had to be made. To Great-grandfather, it was a sad parting, and it seemed a long, long journey—all the way across a great ocean, and to the other side of the globe.

"You shall get a letter from me every fortnight," Frederick promised. "And faster than any letter can go, you shall hear from me by telegraph. The days will be like hours, and the hours like minutes."

By telegraph we received Frederick's greeting to us from England, just as he boarded the steamship. Sooner than any letter could reach us, even though the swift sailing clouds had been our postman, came greetings from America, where Frederick had landed only a few hours before.

"What a glorious and divine inspiration has been granted our age," said Great-grandfather. "It is a true blessing to the human race."

"And it was in our country," I said, "that the natural principle underlying the telegraph was first understood and stated. Frederick told me so."

"Yes," Great-grandfather said, and he kissed me. "Yes, and I once looked into the kindly eyes that were the first to see and understand this marvelous law of nature—his were the eyes of a child, like yours—and I have shaken his hand." Then he kissed me again.

More than a month had gone by, when a letter came from Frederick with the news that he was engaged to a beautiful and lovable young lady. He was sure that everyone in our family would be delighted with her, and he sent us her photograph. We looked at it first with our bare eyes, and then with a magnifying glass, for the advantage of photographs is not only that they stand close inspection through the strongest glass, but that then you see the full likeness even better. No painter has ever been able to do that, even in the greatest of the ages past.

"If only this discovery had been made earlier, then we could have seen the world's greatest and most illustrious men, face to face. How gentle and good this young girl looks," Great-grandfather said, and stared through the glass.

"Now I know her face, and I shall recognize her the moment she comes in the door." But that very nearly failed to happen. Fortunately, at home we did not hear of the danger until it had passed.

After a safe and pleasant trip, the young couple reached England. From there, they were to come by steamship to Copenhagen. When they came in sight of the Danish coast—the white sand dunes along the western shore of Jutland—a heavy sea arose and dashed the ship against the shore. The enormous waves threatened to break the grounded ship in pieces.

No lifeboat could reach them. Night fell, but out of the darkness burst a brightly flashing rocket from the shore. It shot far out over the grounded ship and brought a line to those on board. Once this connection between ship and shore was made fast, a rescue buoy was carefully drawn through the rough, tumultuous sea, to the shore. In it was a lovely young woman, safe and sound, and marvelously happy when she and her young husband again stood together on the shore. Every soul on board was saved before the break of day.

Here in Copenhagen we were sound asleep, dreaming neither of grief nor of danger. When we were gathered at the breakfast table, we heard a rumor that an English steamship had been wrecked on the west coast. We grew heartsick with anxiety, but within an hour we received a telegram from those who were dear to us. Frederick and his young bride were saved—they would soon be with us.

Everyone cried, and I cried too. Great-grandfather cried and clasped his hands. I am sure he gave thanks for the age in which we live, for that very day he gave two hundred dollars toward raising a monument to Hans Christian Oersted. When Frederick came home with his bride, and heard of it, he said, “That was right, Great-grandfather. Now let me read to you what Oersted wrote, a great many years ago, about the old times and the new.”

THE GREAT SEA SERPENT (1871)

There was a little sea fish of good family, the name of which I don't remember; that the more learned will have to tell you. This little fish had eighteen hundred brothers and sisters, all the same age; they didn't know their father or mother, so they had to care for themselves and swim about on their own, but that was a lot of fun. They had plenty of water to drink—the entire ocean. They didn't think about their food; that was sure to come their way. Each did as he pleased; each would have his own story, but then none of them thought about that.

The sun shone down into the water, making it light and clear. It was a world full of the strangest creatures, some of them enormously big, with great, horrible mouths that could sallow all the eighteen hundred brothers and sisters, but none of them thought about that, either, for none of them had ever been swallowed.

The little ones swam together, close to one another, as the herring and the mackerel swim. As they were swimming along at their best and thinking of nothing in particular, there sank from above, down into the midst of them, with a terrifying noise, a long, heavy thing which seemed to have no end to it; further and further it stretched out, and every one of the small fish that it struck was crushed or got a crack from which he couldn't recover. All the fishes, the small and the big as well, were thrown into a panic. That heavy, horrible thing sank deeper and deeper and grew longer and longer, extending for miles—through the entire ocean. Fishes and snails, everything that swims, everything that creeps or is driven by the currents, saw this fearful thing, this enormous unknown sea eel that all of a sudden had come from above.

What kind of thing was it? Yes, we know! It was the great telegraph cable that people were laying between Europe and America.

There were great fear and commotion among all the rightful inhabitants of the ocean where the cable was laid. The flying fish shot up above the surface as high as he could, and the blowfish sped off like a gunshot across the water, for it can do that; other fishes went to the bottom of the ocean with such haste that they reached it long before the telegraph cable was seen down there, and they scared both the codfish and the flounder, who lived peacefully at the bottom of the ocean and ate their neighbors. A couple of the starfish were so frightened that they turned their stomachs inside out, but in spite of that they lived, for they can do that. Many of the lobsters and crabs got out of their fine shells and had to leave their legs behind.

In all this fright and confusion, the eighteen hundred brothers and sisters had all become separated, never again to know or even meet each other, excepting ten of them who had remained at the same place; and after these had held themselves still for a couple of hours, they recovered from their first fright and began to be curious. They looked about; they looked up and they looked down, and there in the deep they thought they saw the frightful thing that had scared them, scared everyone, big and little. There it lay along the bottom of the ocean, extending as far as they could see; it was quite thin, but then they didn't know how thick it could make itself or how strong it was. It lay very quiet, but that, they thought, could be a trick.

"Let it lie where it is! It doesn't concern us," said the most cautious of the little fish. But the very smallest one of them insisted on gaining some knowledge as to what that thing might be. It had come down from above, so above one could best find out about it.

And so they swam up to the surface, where there was calm weather. There they met a dolphin, which is a sort of jumping jack, an ocean rover, that can turn somersaults in the water. As these have eyes to see with, he must have seen what had happened and should know all about it. They inquired, but the dolphin had only been thinking of himself and his somersaults, had seen nothing, and didn't know what to answer, so he kept quiet and looked proud.

Thereupon they turned to the seal who had just ducked down; he was more polite, although seals eat small fishes, for today he had had his fill. He knew a little more than the dolphin.

"Many a night I have rested on a wet rock and looked far inland, miles away from here; there live some sneaky creatures who, in their language, are called people; they plot against us, but often we slip away from them, which I know how to do, and that is what the sea eel has done, too. He has been in their power, up there on the earth, for a long, long time, and from there they carried him off on a ship to bring him across the ocean to a distant land. I saw what trouble they had, but they could manage him, because he had become weak on the earth. They laid him down in coils and circles; I heard how he 'ringled' and 'rangled' when they put him down, but still he got away from them. They held onto him with all their might; many hands held fast, but still he slipped away from them and reached the bottom; there he lies now, for a while at least, I think."

"He is rather thin!" said all the little fish. "They have starved him," said the seal, "but he will soon be himself again, fat and big around. I suppose he is the great sea serpent that people are so afraid of and talk so much about. I had never seen him before and never believed he existed, but now I do; I'm sure he's the sea serpent!" And with that the seal dove down.

"How much he knew! How much he talked!" said all the little fish. "We have never been so enlightened before! If only it isn't all a lie!"

"We could swim down and investigate," said the smallest fish. "On the way, we can hear what others think about it."

"We're not going to move a fin to find out anything more!" said the others, and swam away.

"But I'm going to," said the smallest, and plunged down into deep water.

But the little fish was a considerable distance from the place where "that long sunken thing" lay. He looked and searched in a direction down in the deep water. Never before had he imagined the world to be so big. The herring swam in great masses, each school of them shining like a mighty boat of silver; the mackerel also swam together and looked even more magnificent. There were fishes of all shapes and with markings in all colors. Jellyfish, like half-transparent flowers, simply lay back and let the currents carry them along. Great plants grew up from the bottom of the ocean, as did fathom-high grass and palm-shaped trees, every leaf beset with shining shellfish.

At last the little fish saw a long, dark streak way down and swam toward it; but it was neither fish nor cable; it was the gunwale of a large sunken vessel, the upper and lower decks of which had been broken in two by the force of the ocean. The little fish swam inside, where the many people who had perished with the sinking of the ship had since been washed away, except for two—a young woman lay stretched out with a little child in her arms. The water rocked them to and fro, and they seemed to be asleep. The little fish became quite frightened, for he didn't know that they never again could awaken. Seaweed hung like cultivated foliage over the rail above the fair forms of mother and child. It was so quiet there, so lonely. The little fish hurried away as fast as he could, out to where the water was clearer and there were fishes to see. He hadn't gone far when he met a young and terribly large whale.

"Don't swallow me!" said the little fish. "I'm so small that I'm not even a tiny bite, and it's a great pleasure for me to live!"

"What do you want way down here, where your kind never comes?" asked the whale.

So the little fish told of the strange long eel, or whatever that thing was, which had sunk and scared even the most courageous of ocean creatures.

"Ho, ho!" said the whale, and drew in such a lot of water that he had to make an enormous waterspout when he came to the surface for a breath. "Ho, ho!" he said, "so that was the thing that tickled my back when I turned around! I thought it was a ship's mast that I could use for a back scratcher! However, it wasn't in this location; no, that thing is much farther out. I'll investigate it, though; I have nothing else to do."

And so he swam forth, the little fish following, but not too close, for there would be a powerful stream where the big whale shot through the water.

They met a shark and an old sawfish. These two had also heard of the strange sea eel that was so long and thin; they hadn't seen it, but they wanted to.

Then a catfish appeared. "I'm coming with you!" he said, and took the same course. "If the great sea serpent isn't thicker than a cable, then I'll bite it in two with one bite!" And he opened his mouth and showed his six rows of teeth. "I can bite dents in a ship's anchor, so I can easily bite through that stem!"

"There it is!" said the big whale. "I can see it!" He thought he saw better than the others. "See how it rises, see how it sways, bends, and curves!"

However, this was not the sea serpent, but an exceptionally large eel, who was many yards long, and came closer.

"I've seen him before," said the sawfish. "He's never made much fuss in the ocean here or frightened any big fishes."

And so they talked to him about the new eel and asked if he wanted to join them on their voyage of discovery.

"If that eel is longer than I," said the sea eel, "then something unfortunate will happen."

"That it will!" said the others. "There are enough of us not to have to tolerate it." And then they hurried along.

But now, directly in their way, there appeared a strange monster, bigger than them all. It looked like a floating island that could not hold itself up. It was a very old whale. His head was overgrown with seaweed, his back beset with barnacles and so many oysters and mussels that his black skin was entirely covered with white spots.

"Come along, old fellow," they said. "A new fish has come that we will not tolerate!"

"I'd rather lie where I am," said the old whale. "Leave me in peace. Let me lie. Oh, my, oh, my! I suffer from a dreadful sickness. The only relief I have is when I go up to the surface and get my back above it; then the big, nice birds come and pick at me, and that feels so good, as long they don't drive their beaks in too far; often they go right into my blubber. Just see for yourself! There is a complete skeleton of a bird stuck in my back. That bird struck his claws in too deep and couldn't get loose when I went down to the bottom. Now the little fishes have eaten him. Just see how he looks, and how I look! I have a sickness!"

"That's just imagination!" said the other whale. "I am never sick. No fish is sick!"

"I beg your pardon!" said the old whale. "The eel has a skin disease, the carp has smallpox, and all of us have intestinal worms!"

"Nonsense!" said the shark, and didn't care to hear more; nor did the others; they had something else to do.

Finally, they came to the place where the telegraph cable lay. It had a very long resting place indeed at the bottom of the ocean, from Europe to America, over sandbanks and sea mud, rocky formations and sea-plant wilderness, and, yes, entire forests of coral. The currents down there change, and whirlpools twist around; fishes crowd each other and swim in flocks greater than the countless multitudes of birds that people see when birds of passage are in flight. There are a commotion, a splashing, a humming, and a rushing; a little of that rushing still remains to haunt the big, empty conch shells when we hold them to our ears.

Yes, now they came to the place. "There lies the animal!"

said the big fishes, and the little one said so, too.

They saw the cable, its beginning and end beyond their horizon. Sponges, polyps, and seaweed swayed from the ground, rising and falling over the cable, so that now it was hidden and then visible again. Sea porcupines, snails, and worms moved over it. Gigantic spiders, with whole fringes of vermin on them, crawled along the cable. Dark-blue "sea sausages," or whatever the creatures are called that eat with their entire bodies, lay beside it and smelled this new animal that had come down to lie at the bottom of the ocean. Flounders and codfish turned about in the water, in order to hear what was said from all sides. The starfish, who could hold himself down in the mud and keep his eyes outside, lay and stared to see what would come of all this confusion. The telegraph cable lay motionless. But life and thought were in it; human thoughts went through it.

"That thing is cunning," said the whale. "It's able to hit me in the stomach, and that's my weak point!"

"Let's feel our way," said a polyp. "I have long arms; I have limber fingers. I have touched it. Now I'll feel it a little more firmly." And then he stretched his longest and most flexible arms down to the cable and around it. "It has no scales!" said the polyp. "It has no skin! I don't believe it will ever bear young ones!"

The sea eel laid down alongside the telegraph cable and stretched himself as far as he could. "That thing is longer than I am!" he said. "But it isn't length that counts; one must have skin, stomach, and flexibility!" The whale—that is, the young, strong whale—dove down deeper than he ever had been. "Are you a fish or a plant?" he asked the cable. "Or are you only some piece of work from above that can't thrive down here among us?"

But the telegraph cable didn't answer; it had no means of contacting anyone at such a location. Thoughts were going through it, people's thoughts, which in a single second were heard from land to land, many hundreds of miles apart.

"Will you answer, or do you want to be broken?" asked the fierce shark, and all the other big fishes asked the same. "Will you answer, or do you want to be broken?"

The cable didn't move, but it had its own private thoughts, which it had a right to have, considering that it was filled with other's thoughts. "Let them break me; then I'll be hauled up and put in order again—that has happened to others of my kind who were in shallower waters." And so it didn't answer; it had something else to do; it telegraphed and thereby did its just duty at the bottom of the sea.

Up above, the sun was going down, as people say. It blazed like the reddest fire, and all the clouds in the heavens glowed with a fiery hue, each more magnificent than the other.

"Now we're getting the red lighting," said the polyps, "and we may be able to see the thing better, if necessary."

"At it! At it!" shouted the shark, showing all his teeth.

"At it! At it!" said the swordfish, and the whale, and the sea eel. They rushed forward, the shark leading, but just as he was about to bite the cable, the swordfish, out of pure anxiety, ran his saw right into the back of the shark; that was a great mistake, and the shark had no strength left to bite. Everything became muddled in the mud. Big fishes, little fishes, "sea sausages," and snails ran into one another, ate each other—clashed and gnashed. The cable lay still and attended to its own business, as one should do.

The dark night brooded above; but in the ocean the millions and millions of small living creatures lighted it. Crawfish, not even as big as a pinhead, gave out light. It is quite wondrous, but now that's the way it is.

The ocean creatures looked at the telegraph cable. "What is that thing, and what isn't it?" Yes, that was the question.

Presently an old sea cow appeared. People call these mermaids or mermen. This one was a she, and had a tail and two short arms to splash with; she wore seaweed and parasites over her breasts and head, and she was proud of this.

"Are you seeking knowledge and wisdom?" she said. "I am the only one who can give you this; but in return I demand that you guarantee safe pasturage on the bottom of the ocean for me and mine. I am a fish like you are, but I am also a crawling animal, through practice. I am the wisest in the ocean; I know about everything that moves down here and about all that goes on up above. That thing you are pondering over is from above, and whatever falls down from up there is dead, or will be dead, and powerless; let it lie there for what it is. It's only a man-made invention."

"I believe there is more to it than that!" said the little fish.

"Hold your tongue, mackerel!" said the big sea cow.

"Stickleback!" said the others, and that was even more insulting.

And the sea cow explained further to them that this alarming thing, which, as a matter of fact, hadn't uttered a single sound, was in its entirety nothing more than some new device from the dry land, and she delivered a little lecture about people's deceitfulness. "They want to catch us," she said; "that's all they live for. They stretch out nets for us, and come with bait on hooks to tempt us. That thing there is some sort of big string that they think we are going to bite. They are so stupid! But we are not! Don't touch that junk; in time it will unravel and all turn to dust and mud. Everything that comes from up there cracks and breaks—is good for nothing!"

"Good for nothing!" said the other ocean creatures, and held onto the sea cow's opinion, so as to have an opinion.

The little fish, however, had his own thoughts. "Perhaps that enormously long, thin serpent is the most wonderful fish in the ocean. I have a feeling it is."

"The most wonderful," say we humans, too, and we say it with knowledge and assurance.

The great sea serpent has long been the theme of song and story. It was conceived and born by man's ingenuity and laid on the bottom of the ocean, stretching from the eastern to the western lands, and carrying messages as swiftly as light flashes from the sun to our earth. It grows, grows in power and length, grows year after year, through all oceans, around the world; it is beneath the stormy seas and the glass-clear waters, where the skipper, as if sailing through transparent air, looks down and sees crowds of fishes resembling many-colored fireworks.

Deepest down of all lies the outstretched serpent, a blessed Midgard snake, which bites its own tail as it encircles Earth. Fishes and other sea creatures clash with it; they do not understand that thing from above. People's thoughts rush noiselessly, in all languages, through the serpent of science, for both good and evil; the most wondrous of the ocean's wonders is our time's—

GREAT SEA SERPENT.

"DANCE, DANCE, DOLL OF MINE!" (1871)

Yes, this is a song for very small children!" declared Aunt Malle. "As much as I should like to, I cannot follow this 'Dance, Dance, Doll of Mine!'"

But little Amalie could; she was only three years old, played with dolls, and brought them up to be just as wise as Aunt Malle.

There was a student who came to the house to help her brothers with their lessons, and he frequently spoke to little Amalie and her dolls; he spoke differently from anyone else, and the little girl found him very amusing, although Aunt Malle said he didn't know how to converse with children—their little heads couldn't possibly grasp that silly talk. But little Amalie did. Yes, the student even taught her the whole song, "Dance, Dance, Doll of Mine!" and she sang it to her three dolls; two were new, one a girl doll and the other a boy doll, but the third doll was old; her name was Lise-moér. She also heard the song, and was even in it.

Dance, dance, doll of mine!
Girl doll's dress is very fine.
Boy doll is a dandy, too;
He wears gloves and hat and shoe;
White pants, blue coat, him adorn;
On his toe he has a corn.
He is fine and she is fine.
Dance, dance, doll of mine!

Old doll's name is Lise-moér;
She is from the year before;
Hair is new; it's made of flax,
Forehead polished up with wax.
Young again, not old and done.
Come along, my cherished one,
Let us dance a fast gavotte;
To watch it is worth a lot.
Dance, dance, doll of mine!
Watch your steps and get in line;
One foot forward; watch your feet.
Dancing makes you slender, sweet.
Bow and twist and turn around;
That will make you hale and sound.
What a sight it is to see!
You are doing fine, all three.

And the dolls understood the song; little Amalie understood it, and so did the student, but then he had written it himself and said it was excellent. Only Aunt Malle didn't understand it; she had passed over the fence of youth. "Silly song!" she said.

But not little Amalie! She sings it. It is from her that we know it.